Teacher Workload

Teacher Workload

Primary Recommendations for Improvement

M. Scott Norton

ROWMAN & LITTLEFIELD
Lanham • Boulder • New York • London

Published by Rowman & Littlefield
An imprint of The Rowman & Littlefield Publishing Group, Inc.
4501 Forbes Boulevard, Suite 200, Lanham, Maryland 20706
www.rowman.com

86-90 Paul Street, London EC2A 4NE

Copyright © 2021 by M. Scott Norton

All rights reserved. No part of this book may be reproduced in any form or by any electronic or mechanical means, including information storage and retrieval systems, without written permission from the publisher, except by a reviewer who may quote passages in a review.

British Library Cataloguing in Publication Information Available

Library of Congress Cataloging-in-Publication Data

Names: Norton, M. Scott, author.
Title: Teacher workload : primary recommendations for improvement / M. Scott Norton.
Description: Lanham : Rowman & Littlefield, [2021] | Includes bibliographical references. | Summary: "How to measure teacher workload and make necessary load adjustments are set forth in various strategies and innovative programming"— Provided by publisher.
Identifiers: LCCN 2021035453 (print) | LCCN 2021035454 (ebook) | ISBN 9781475861198 (Cloth) | ISBN 9781475861204 (Paperback) | ISBN 9781475861211 (eBook)
Subjects: LCSH: Teachers—Workload—United States. | Teachers—Time management. | Classroom management.
Classification: LCC LB2844.1.W6 N65 2021 (print) | LCC LB2844.1.W6 (ebook) | DDC 371.14/12—dc23
LC record available at https://lccn.loc.gov/2021035453
LC ebook record available at https://lccn.loc.gov/2021035454

Contents

Preface ... vii

1 The Factors, Conditions, and Activities that Constitute a Teacher's Workload ... 1

2 Calculating and Assessing the Workload of Teacher Personnel ... 27

3 School Climate and Its Influence on Teacher Workload ... 53

4 The Primary Recommendations for Improving Teacher Workload ... 73

About the Author ... 95

Preface

WHY THIS BOOK WAS WRITTEN

Teacher workload has been a historical problem in education that has accelerated due to the present problems of the COVID-19 epidemic. Studies of teacher workload have revealed the fact that the heaviest workloads commonly have been held by new teachers and those teachers who have been evaluated as the best teachers in the school.

The outcomes of these findings are revealed in the growing numbers of teachers that leave the profession along with the difficulties of encouraging talented personnel to enter the profession of education. For example, if 50 new teachers were hired within a school district, after their first year of teaching, 15% to 20% of these teachers will not continue to teach a second year. Additionally, 50% of these teachers will leave the profession within five years in the schoolroom.

The high expense and expended effort of helping these teachers to become part of the school system are lost. The impact of the virus epidemic has had a negative effect on the ability to hire and retain teacher personnel. In addition, both veteran and new teachers, in many school districts across the nation, have decided not to return to their school positions most directly due to the effects of closed schools and the COVID-19 epidemic that affects both students and adults.

As noted in various responsible reports, school districts are finding it impossible to hire needed personnel and too many individuals, who previously held interests in the teaching profession, are changing their career aspirations.

This book focuses on the primary factors that are causing teacher workload problems. It becomes clear that the factor of class size is only one such factor and that many other factors/conditions in the school system make up the heavy workloads that lead to teacher loss.

HOW THIS BOOK IS ORGANIZED

Chapter 1 of the book sets the stage for understanding the importance of teacher load in education and its history of problems related to inequality of work assignments and its effects on student learning. The importance of the effects of the virus pandemic on educational practices is kept in mind as well as the problems that come about due to the closing and reopening of schools. Chapter 2 gives special attention to how teacher load has been allocated historically and the inequities that teacher work assignments have reduced the positive effects of quality teaching.

Chapter 3 gives primary attention to the "best" practices that have been recommended for improving teacher load inequities and sometimes implemented in school districts nationally during the pandemic. Just how these practices have proven effective has yet to be determined. Schools have closed, reopened, and sometimes closed once again.

Chapter 4 centers on the many and various "solutions" that have been implemented in school districts. The variances of student attendance, teacher absenteeism, and the inability to "hire" a sufficient teaching staff in many school districts continue to exist.

The book's information is all-inclusive in that it sets forth the major problems being faced by school districts nationally. Unfortunately, although the book includes a high volume of "best practices" recommended for improving teacher workload, the actual positive effects on student learning have been talked about but not thoroughly researched. So many different school districts are doing many different things making a large sampling of the program methods somewhat difficult.

Teachers and school administrators will find the book of great interest during the pandemic and also of value after the pandemic has been resolved. College and university personnel, who are in the various areas of education, will find the work of interest and value as well. Practicing educational personnel will find the information regarding "best practices" of special interest. Members of school boards will find the book's contents of special value in helping to develop school district policies and administrative regulations relative to personnel administration and teacher work assignments. To date, basic research on instructional practices during the pandemic has been limited at best.

Chapter 1

The Factors, Conditions, and Activities that Constitute a Teacher's Workload

Primary chapter goal: To investigate the topic of teacher workload—what it is and why it ranks so high as a major educational problem nationally and to examine the effects of the virus pandemic on the workload of teachers.

TEACHERS HAVE INCREASINGLY HEAVY WORKLOADS—SO WHAT?

With the exception of the worldwide COVID-19 pandemic, the financial support of education and the problem of increasing teacher workload constitute the major problems facing our nation's schools. Without solutions to these two serious matters, education for children and youth in America will continue to be ranked as only "average" among the other nations of the world.

Santry (2019) reported that more than 25% of teachers and school leaders were thinking of leaving the profession in the next few months. The reason for such action was primarily due to excessive workloads being encountered. That is, new teachers were quitting because they found that workloads were much worse than expected. Nearly three-quarters of the teachers were working over contracted hours. Prospective teachers were losing interest in education as a major profession.

So, the major educational problems of teacher availability, teacher retention, and teacher workload continue to wane toward the bottom of America's list of problems to resolve. However, perhaps the "biggest" surprise of all, in regard to the matter of teacher workload, is the "volume" of empirical research that continues to be devoted to the topic. Empirical research, of course, has centered more on matters related to the problems of teacher workload rather than on the actions needed for their resolution. The problems of COVID-19, global warming, the rising national debt, legal voting, and others have been headline-news most recently. The problem of teacher workload has reached the news headlines and has been the title of many articles in various professional journals.

THE COVID-19 EPIDEMIC AND ITS IMPACT ON EDUCATION GENERALLY AND TEACHER LOAD SPECIFICALLY

The serious loss of professional personnel in education has been accelerated due to the present problems related to COVID-19. Yet, the serious loss was occurring long before the pandemic came upon the scene. Even before the pandemic, fewer individuals were entering preparation programs for teacher licensing and the loss of practicing teacher personnel was ongoing. Teacher load is not a condition that has just arrived on the American educational scene. It has been an inhibiting factor of effective student learning for many decades. This fact is the main focus of chapter 1.

During the current "explosion" of COVID-19 in America and around the world, schools in America are being tossed back and forth, opened and closed, then opened and closed again. In the meantime, quality education in America goes wanting. Homeschooling strategies have been minimally effective at best. Many teachers have refused to return to the school environment. In addition, teacher preparation programs are wanting for potential teacher candidates. The virus continues to spread.

One report by Stroud (2017) voiced the thoughts of one teacher who commented that "I'm not going to teach, I can't face the thought of so much work and all that stress." Another teacher said, "I'm not sure how much longer I can do this." It has long been known that the annual turnover of teacher personnel has had a negative effect on the learning program for children and youth. The question to be posed and answered is, "What actually makes up what is it that the teacher might not be able to do any longer?".

When we witness the loss of 20% of first-year teachers each and every year, apparently, we resolve the problem in our own minds by saying, "Well, that's just the way it is in education." Rather than working to find the best solutions for solving the ongoing teacher shortage, we implement temporary "solutions" by increasing class sizes, hiring unlicensed personnel to teach, reducing the expansion of educational classes/activities for students, and increasing the workloads for the faculty personnel and others who work in the schools.

MISCONCEPTIONS OF THE TERM "TEACHER LOAD"

When one hears the term "teacher load," it most commonly is viewed as being synonymous with the term "class size." Although the number of students in the class is one component of teacher load, it is only one of the several factors that make up the workload of the teacher. It is somewhat surprising, that over the years, many formulas have been set forth for the purpose of measuring teacher load. For example, almost 90 years ago, Almack and Bursch (1931) set forth a teacher load formula that considered the four workload components of class periods taught, number of pupils taught, cooperative duties required, and the nature of the subject taught.

HISTORICAL STUDIES OF TEACHER LOAD

As early as 1922, F. H. Koos completed a survey of the loads of 236 Minnesota high school teachers. He measured the time spent in various activities connected with their work during the week and found that the total day's work averaged 8.61 hours. Another important finding was that some teachers were overloaded with too much nonteaching work revealed in too much routine. Workload survey research has been ongoing since this early time in history.

Koos suggested that the loads of some of the teachers be increased and some should be decreased according to the subject being taught. He noted also that too much time was being spent on athletics and that time could be better spent on valuable work such as public speaking, dramatics, the school newspaper, and social activities. It was Koos's opinion that the teacher needed to spend more time in professional development, reading, and training to prevent professional stagnation. Keep in mind that Koos's recommendations were set forth nearly 100 years ago. The Douglass's teacher load formula for secondary schools was established approximately 30 years later.

Another early study was set forth by Davis in 1923. Davis's study included 1,100 high school teachers in 100 public high schools. Davis's study is of special importance due to its load findings that appear to be duplicated in most every load study developed since that time. Davis made the following conclusion:

> The most important determinants of the teaching load are the "personality" of the class taught, the number of different preparations required for class work daily, the number of classes taught daily, the amount of clerical work connected with the teaching process, the extra-curricular and extra-classroom school duties of the teacher, and the social and civic demands on the teacher. (p. 3)

Table 1.1 1923, the Typical Teacher's Day 100 Years Ago

Typical Teacher's Daily Activities	Number of Minutes
Preparing two or three distinct recitation lessons	60
Teaching five 45-minute classes	225
Correcting papers, themes, etc.	45
Keeping students after school hours	30
Assisting in collateral pupil-activities	30
Performing other delegated school duties	90
Engaging in private professional reading	30
Engaging in other voluntary professional study	0
Sleeping	480
Going to and from school	40
At meals	75
Reading for pleasure	40
Physical recreation	30
Social recreation	40
In religious and charitable work	5
In civic work	0
In home duties	220
Total	1,440 minutes (24 hrs.)

It is interesting to note Davis's final conclusion regarding the typical teacher's time spent during the 24 hours of a day. Table 1.1 presents the results of this early 1923 workload study. Do any of these nearly 100-year-old teacher activities conjure up any contemporary workload characteristics?

TEACHER PREPARATION AND EARLY TEACHER INSTITUTES

It was in the early 1840s when Henry Barnard, then the state school superintendent in Connecticut, called upon the state legislature to fund teacher institutes to increase the competence of beginning teachers in the state. The state legislature refused to do so. Barnard, one of the nation's leading educators of the time, paid for the implementation of the first teacher institutes himself.

The purpose of the teacher institutes was briefly stated as "being three-day meetings at which he and others taught lessons on the basics, globes and school keeping" (Bloss, 1882). From this initiative, county township institutes developed around the country. Ultimately, these institutes gave way to the revolutionary *normal school* whereby aspiring teachers could be "licensed" after two full years of educational training.

In the middle years of the 1800s, normal schools opened within the states. The implementation of teacher colleges, that offered four-year teaching degrees, were soon to follow. The name, Teacher's College, changed over the years to

Table 1.2 Item Analysis of Teaching Load Formulas. Factors in Determining Teacher's Load as Proposed by Various Authors over the Years

	Class Periods,	Dup. Assignments,	No. of Preps,	No. of Pupils,	Coope-ration,	Period Length,	Subject Wt.,	Stand. Teach Load
Almack-Bursch 1931	X			X	X	X		
Pauly 1935	X			X	X			
Phil. P. S. 1936	X				X			
Ward 1936	X		X	X	X	X		
Middle States Assoc. 1937	X			X		X		
Frost 1941	X		X	X		X		X
Cinn. F.S. 1944	X			X		X		
Garland 1944	X				X			
Douglass 1950	X	X	X	X	X	X	X	X
Clark 1954	X				X	X		
Brown & Fritzmeier	X			X	X	X	X	X
Abraham	X							X
Harrington	X							X
Hutson	X			X	X			
'woody-Bergman	X						X	X
Sand	X	X		X	X			
Mees	X	X		X	X	X		
Pettit	X			X	X	X		
Davis	X			X	X	X		
Baer	X			X		X		

Norton/Bria, 1992 (see the following paragraph for this formula's load factors)

the more contemporary name of the *College of Education.* Teacher colleges implemented four-year education programs for students aspiring to the education profession. Many teachers went on to earn a master's degree in education. However, a large percentage of these master's degrees were recorded as majors in educational administration as opposed to elementary or secondary education.

Table 1.2 shows the item analysis of teaching load formulas. The exact date in which each of the formulas were developed is not known in all instances. Fifteen teaching load formulas are identified with one formula by Almack and Bursch being set forth nearly 90 years ago.

A HISTORY OF TEACHER LOAD FORMULAS

It comes as a surprise to many persons when they learn of the efforts to develop a means of "measuring" teacher load as early as 1931; that is nearly 90 years ago. Table 1.2 sets forth a collection of 21 teacher load formulas that have been developed over the years. Table 1.2 identifies the load components that were included in each of the several formulas. Over the years, the Douglas Teacher Load Formula has been most commonly used to measure teacher load in the nation's secondary schools. As indicated by the information in Table 1.2, the Douglass formula includes eight primary load factors including class periods taught, duplicate assignments, number of preparations, number of pupils, cooperative duties, length of class periods, the subject weight factor, and the standard load factor. A teacher load formula for elementary school teachers was developed by Norton/Bria in 1992. The components of the formula differ from earlier formulas for secondary schools in several ways. For example, the Norton/Bria formula served to calculate the actual hours of time that the teacher spent on the job weekly. The time factor was calculated by determining the assigned teaching hours spent in the classroom per week, the time spent in class preparation, the number of students being taught above or below the average class size for any given grade, the time devoted to assigned cooperative duties, and the consideration for the time spent for added load activities for a teacher who has to teach two grades in any one classroom.

According to Norton, the Norton/Bria formula could be improved by research that served to determine the Grade Level Coefficient (GLC) for K-6 grade levels. That is, which grade levels require more time to prepare, present, and follow-up, if any?

It will be noted in the Douglas Teacher Load Formula that a Subject Grade Coefficient (SGC) was established that gives some subjects "credit" for requiring more time and effort on preparation and related student activities. An SGC of number one was determined as being the common credit for such courses as mathematics, business, and social studies. Chemistry, home economics, physics, agriculture, and vocational education each held higher SGCs. The complete Douglas Teacher Load Formula is developed later in chapter 2. The components of the formula, as well as examples of its application in practice, are discussed in depth in chapter 2. In addition, the Norton/Bria Elementary School Teacher Load Formula and its applications are presented in the next chapter as well.

THE ESTABLISHMENT OF OFFICIAL POLICIES FOR SCHOOL ACCREDITATION

Historically, the North Central Association of Colleges and Secondary Schools, as well as accrediting agencies in various sections of the country, establish certain policies, regulations, and criteria for the approval of colleges and secondary schools. It investigates applicant schools within the North

Central Association, sets as an accreditation agency, and prepares an annual list of accredited secondary schools and colleges.

One early regulation serves to explain the standards on teaching load as approved by the Association. That regulation is stated as follows:

> In determining the teaching load, consideration is given to the following components: The number of periods of class teaching, the number of different preparations, study hall duty, class size, total number of pupils taught daily, the demands made in the way of guidance and supervisory activities, and duties involved in the sponsorship of pupil activities. Due allowance is made in computing the teacher load for special assignments in committee work whose purpose is to improve any phase of the school program. (North Central Association of Colleges and Secondary Schools, 1958)

In addition, the foregoing regulation also stated that a teaching load in excess of seven periods daily, including study hall and assignments, is considered as a violation of the foregoing regulation. An average enrollment in the school in excess of thirty pupils per teacher is considered as a violation of the regulation. These factors have been considered as being "standards" for teacher load most for many years.

Some differences among the several accreditation agencies in the country continue to exist. For example, the North Central Association at one time expressed the policy that a pupil-teacher ratio of 25 to 1 was appropriate. The New England Association recommended a 30 to 1 ratio but did view this number as being a limit.

An attempt to determine just how the student-teacher ratio was being addressed during the virus pandemic proved to be most difficult.

TEACHERS' WORKLOADS ARE ALL ALIKE, OR ARE THEY?

Empirical research has revealed that some teachers are carrying workloads twice the "size" of other teachers. In fact, Norton's (1959) early study of teacher workload set forth statistics that showed new teachers in some schools were carrying load assignments twice the weight indices of other teachers. In addition, those individuals that were evaluated as being "best" teachers and those individuals in their first year of teaching were found to be carrying the heaviest workloads in the majority of schools. Should we be surprised that these teachers commonly leave the classroom after their first year of teaching or that a large percentage of them opt out of the profession altogether after their fifth year in the classroom?

School districts that want to attract and retain quality personnel will have to do so strategically. Efforts must be deliberate, well thought out, and specifically focused. We must look at the personnel function in new and different ways. It means that we must look at the recruitment of teachers differently, and at the assignment of teachers in increasingly creative ways. This topic is considered in-depth in later chapters of the book.

EFFORTS IMPLEMENTED IN AN ATTEMPT TO RETAIN TEACHER PERSONNEL

It is through these kinds of personnel practices that bonding between the teacher and the school is enhanced. How might this be achieved? One recommended strategy is the use of a retention questionnaire that serves to ascertain the employee's in-grade or subject-interest areas changes. Indications of present and/or developing new interest areas must be gathered by the use of such a brief survey instrument such the one that is discussed later in this chapter.

Leslie Chisholm (1953) pinpointed the primary importance of determining equitable assignments of teacher load. He set forth the following warning more than six decades ago. Chisholm stated that "unless the responsibility for an equitable assignment of duties among the teachers is kept in mind, it will be significantly violated. . . . The net result is that those who are best equipped to contribute the greatest among in carrying on the effective educational program in the school are so overburdened that their efforts often are forced to a level of actual mediocrity" (468–69).

THE NEED TO REASSESS THE SCHOOL DISTRICT'S PERSONNEL PRACTICES

Teacher loss, for example, has to be attributed in part to shortsighted recruitment and selection practices. Recruiters have tended to focus on the single task of selecting candidates to satisfy the school district's goals of filling a vacancy without giving attention to the candidate's aspirations.

Such attention can be implemented by asking questions such as the following: What goals and objectives does the teacher candidate have in mind? What does the candidate really want out of the position in question? Does the school environment match or provide realistic opportunities to match these objectives? Can the career goals of the candidate be met in the school district overtime? If not, there is a high likelihood that there will be a mismatch and the employee will be unable to form a bond with the school district.

If the school hires mismatches, it is likely that it will result in increasing turnover. Refining the recruitment and selection processes to emphasize "good fit," not merely attracting personnel—such thinking requires that we look for commitment: Does the candidate really want to be a member of the school district for the right reasons? The need is to take a long-term view in the selection of new employees. If recruitment and selection are important, as we know they are, part of the performance appraisal of personnel administrators should be the meeting of teacher retention goals. Retention of quality personnel looms important for many reasons. Administrators are quite likely to give more attention to those goals that are evaluated.

THE HIGH COSTS OF TEACHER TURNOVER

Give thought to the matter of teacher turnover. Various monetary cost figures have been set forth for hiring a teacher; $20,000 has been a common figure. The "cost" on student learning is a major problem to consider. The new teacher's induction into the school takes much time and effort. The school district's costs for "teaching" the new hire about the school and school district's programs and purposes, community relationships, policies and regulations, and the costs of planning and presenting important in-service programs for new personnel, all is lost when the new teacher decides to "call it quits." The school and school district, of course, must do all of the foregoing activities once again for another new hire.

Of course, the historical problem of finding quality teacher personnel faces most every school district in America. As one school administrator commented during a personnel meeting in one school district, "If I even find a teacher candidate that is still warm, I hire them on the spot!" Those in the meeting did join him in the laughter, but the problem of finding potential hires has become increasingly difficult. Without question, the virus pandemic has added greatly to this major problem in America. Thus, teacher retention becomes increasingly important.

WHY PEOPLE LEAVE THEIR POSITIONS?

People leave positions for a variety of reasons. One obvious reason is that of better opportunities. The opportunities for advancement within the school district is one leading factor in the positive retention of quality personnel. Effective professional development programs that tie to specific opportunities for advancement within the school district are of paramount importance. An advancement does not have to be a vertical movement from a teaching position to an assistant principalship.

Teachers leave positions in some instances for better opportunities. One study of 117 companies reported that 39% of the employees left for a better position with another company. Career counseling, as related to career opportunities within the school system, has been identified as one of the top priorities of new faculty. How can school leaders make the grass greener in their own school district?

Or, an individual faculty member might be appointed to an important position of school safety director, coordinator of the reading program, after-school program activities, curriculum coordinator, director of school instructional resources, school newsletter editor, health information leader, parental participation director, head mentor, or other roles in which the teacher is interested and experienced.

One important personnel recommendation is to evaluate the job descriptions of each faculty member in efforts to determine important upgrades in the individual's work assignments. Providing training workshops, personal mentoring, extended education possibilities, and other consultation activities serve to demonstrate the school district's concern and interest in the personal interests and goals of the worker.

Workers are most interested in having a clear development path that leads to their growth and development goals. Some studies have revealed that positive personnel orientation programs, ones that focus on providing personal assistance for meeting the goals of the employee, were among the very best practices for fostering positive job satisfaction for teachers in the profession.

But how do school leaders find out about the special interests and goals of their faculty personnel? Though there are a variety of strategies for doing so, one best way is simply to "ask them." The point primarily is this: the oft-stated principle of "knowing one's staff" goes far beyond just knowing them as a person. Rather, knowing and helping the workers achieve their goals loom important.

WHAT ACTIVITIES, RESPONSIBILITIES, AND ASSIGNMENTS CONSTITUTE THE WORKLOAD OF THE TEACHER?

It was noted previously that the term "workload" commonly is equated with class size. Along with the load factors set forth earlier in table 1.1, other load factors/conditions have entered the load picture today. As one teacher noted, "For the first 5 or 6 years of my teaching career, I worked all the time. I guess I'd just come to accept that a never-ending teacher workload was part of the job. After all, we did get summers off. I worked nights. I worked weekends. Once I pulled an all-nighter so I could get my grades in on time. There was always a big pile of paperwork and a looming deadline. Grade that pile of essays. Enter the homework into the grade book. Call the parent again. Submit my lesson plans two weeks out" (EdSurge News, 2020, p. 1/12).

The teacher continued to point out that all of the foregoing work activities were before COVID-19 and online learning. She noted that during the pandemic, teachers have been asked to do even more. They must redesign learning experiences for students overnight, keep teaching current classes, and pursue field help requests from parents and students, seemingly on a 24/7 schedule. Stress levels and unhealthy life activities serve to interfere with the teacher's quality of work. In addition, it cannot be forgotten that each teacher has personal "home duties" to care for as well. Family responsibilities rank high on the list of teachers' concerns during the ongoing COVID-19 epidemic.

INEQUITIES IN TEACHER ASSIGNMENTS

Empirical research has revealed that workload assignments in schools have been assigned inequitably. In fact, Norton's study (1959) of teacher workload set forth statistics that revealed the fact that new teachers in some schools were carrying load assignments twice the weight indices of other teachers. In addition, those individuals that were evaluated as being "best" teachers and those individuals in their first year of teaching were found to be carrying the heaviest workloads in the majority of schools. Should we be surprised that these teachers commonly leave the classroom after their first year of teaching or that they opt out of the profession altogether after their fifth year in the classroom?

REDUCING TEACHER LOSS WITH IMPROVED PERSONNEL PRACTICES

School districts that need to attract and retain quality personnel will have to do so strategically. That contention means that recruitment and selection efforts must be deliberate, well thought out, and specifically focused. School leaders must look at the personnel function in new and different ways. It means that we must look at the recruitment of teachers differently, and at the assignment of teachers in increasingly creative ways.

DEALING WITH TEACHER RETENTION

Teacher loss, for example, has to be attributed in part to shortsighted recruitment and selection practices. Recruiters have tended to focus on the single task of selecting candidates to satisfy the school district's goals of filling a vacancy without giving attention to the candidate's aspirations. What immediate and long-term goals are in the mind of the candidate? What does the candidate really want out of the position in question? Does the school environment match or provide realistic opportunities to match these objectives? Can the career goals of the candidate be met in the school district overtime? If not, there is a high likelihood that there will be a mismatch and the employee will be unable to form a bond with the school district.

If the school hires mismatches, it is likely that it will result in increasing turnover. Refining the recruitment and selection processes to emphasize "good fit," not merely attracting personnel—such thinking requires that we look for commitment: Does the candidate really want to be a member of the school district for the right reasons? The need is to take a long-term view in the selection of new employees. If recruitment and selection are important, as we know they are, part of the performance appraisal of personnel administrators should be the meeting of teacher retention goals. Retention of quality personnel looms important for many reasons. Administrators are quite likely to give more attention to those goals that are evaluated.

Give thought to the matter of teacher turnover. Various cost figures have been set forth for hiring a teacher; $20,000 has been a common cost figure. The new teacher's induction into the school takes much time and effort. The school district's costs for "teaching" the new hire about the school and school district's programs and purposes, community relationships, policies and regulations, and the costs of planning and presenting important in-service programs for new personnel, all is lost when the new teacher decides to "call it quits." The school and school district, of course, must do all of the foregoing once again for another new hire.

A FOCUS ON TEACHER TURNOVER

Teachers all too often are given assignments that reduce their chances of success. As noted previously, it not uncommon to find that new personnel carry the heaviest teacher loads or are assigned to the least attractive schools in the district. While such an assignment might be justified for various reasons, logic might say that first and second-year teachers would benefit by having loads that are somewhat reduced during these first teaching years. Effective teacher assignments, first of all, place individuals in situations that allow them to soar with their strengths, to pursue their personal interests, and to use their background of experience.

It is through these kinds of personnel practices that bonding between the teacher and the school is enhanced. One strategy for retaining teachers is the use of a retention questionnaire that serves to ascertain the employee's in-grade or subject-interest areas changes. Indications of present and/or developing new interest areas can be easily gathered by the use of such a brief survey instrument such is shown in the following information.

ASSIGNMENT QUESTIONNAIRE AND INTEREST ASSESSMENT

Name of Teacher_____
Present Position_____ Location_____ Grade
                Levels_____Subjects Taught _____
            _____ ____-_____ _____
Time at Present Location_____
Teaching Assignment Change Being Requested:
    Grade Level Change (please explain)_____
    _____
    Subject Area Change (Please explain)_____
    _____
    Supervisory or Extra-Curricular Assignments: Changes requested:
    _____

Comments/Clarifications: _____
    _____
School Principal's Comments/Recommendations: _____
    _____
    _____
    Signature:_____ Date: _____

Variances in the Assignments of Teachers

Empirical research has revealed that some teachers are carrying workloads twice the 'size' of other teachers. As previously noted, Norton's study of teacher workload set forth statistics that showed new teachers in some schools were carrying load assignments twice the weight indices of other teachers. In addition, those individuals that were evaluated as being 'best' teachers and those individuals in their first year of teaching were found to be carrying the heaviest workloads in the majority of schools. Should we be surprised that these teachers commonly leave the classroom after their first year of teaching or they opt out of the profession altogether after their fifth year in the classroom?

School districts that want to attract and retain quality personnel will have to do so strategically. Efforts must be deliberate, well thought out and specifically focused. We must look at the personnel function in new and different ways. It means that we must look at the recruitment of teachers differently, and at the assignment of teachers in increasingly creative ways.

If recruitment and selection are important, as we know they are, part of the performance appraisal of personnel administrators should be the meeting of teacher retention goals. Retention of quality personnel looms important for many reasons. Administrators are quite likely to give more attention to those goals that are evaluated.

A FURTHER LOOK AT TEACHER TURNOVER

Give thought to the matter of teacher turnover. Various cost figures have been set forth for hiring a teacher; $20,000 has been a common figure. The new teacher's induction into the school takes much time and effort. The school district's costs for "teaching" the new hire about the school and school district's programs and purposes, community relationships, policies and regulations, and the costs of planning and presenting important in-service programs for new personnel, all is lost when the new teacher decides to "call it quits." The school and school district, of course, must do all of the foregoing administrative activities once again for recruiting and hiring another new hire.

One important personnel recommendation is to evaluate the job descriptions of each faculty member in efforts to determine important upgrades in the individual's work assignments. Providing training workshops, personal mentoring, extended education possibilities, and other consultation activities serve to demonstrate the school district's concern and interest in the personal interests and goals of the worker.

HOW TO SOLVE THE PROBLEM OF WORK OVERLOAD: ANSWERS FOUND IN THE LITERATURE

Dealing effectively with the negative outcomes of troublesome workloads is addressed seriously in later chapters of this book. However, if you are in a "bigger hurry" to get on with it, several of the "contemporary winners" for reducing your workload follow. Although the following recommendations are set here with some humor in mind, contemporary literature gives some questionable legitimacy to the following recommendations for reducing teacher workload.

Don't aim for perfection, just do the job as you've been doing it; ask for help and learn to say "no"; when things get out of control, get them under control; remember the phrase, "It is what it is" and use it often; list your priorities according to their difficulty and then do the easiest ones first; call in sick; if you find yourself working too many hours, just work fewer hours; when the principal says, "Think of your students," just think of the ones that give you all those dxxx problems; when the school superintendent asks every teacher to give just 10% more, ask him or her if that figure can be applied to your salary increase next year; and lastly, if you just fail to accomplish all the work that is piled on your desk, remember that a person can learn a great deal through his or her failures.

THE PROBLEM OF WORKLOAD HAS ALWAYS BEEN WITH US: DO WE REALLY GIVE A DARN?

Teacher workload has been talked about being a major problem in education for many decades. It was noted previously that the term "workload" commonly is equated with class size. Along with the load factors set forth earlier in table 1.1, other load factors/conditions have entered the load picture today. As one teacher noted (EdSurge News, 2020), "For the first 5 or 6 years of my teaching career, I worked all the time. I guess I'd just come to accept that a never-ending teacher workload was part of the job. After all, we did get summers off. I worked nights. I worked weekends. Once I pulled an all-nighter so I could get my grades in on time. There was always a big pile of paperwork and a looming deadline. Grade that pile of essays. Enter the homework into the grade book. Call the parent again. Submit my lesson plans two weeks out" (p. 1/12).

The teacher goes on to point out that all of the foregoing work activities were before COVID-19 and online learning. She notes that during the pandemic, teachers are asked to do even more. They must redesign learning experiences for students overnight, keep teaching current classes, and pursue field help requests from parents and students, seemingly on a 24/7 schedule.

Stress levels and healthy life activities serve to interfere with the teacher's quality of work. In addition, it cannot be forgotten that each teacher has personal "home duties" to care for as well. It is obvious that workload has become a leading problem regarding the recruitment, hiring, and retention of personnel for work in the public schools.

HOW HAS COVID-19 AFFECTED THE EMOTIONAL LIVES OF TEACHERS?

Cipriano and Brackett (2020, April 7) surveyed over 5,000 U.S. teachers asking them to describe the three most frequent emotions they felt each day during the COVID-19 crisis. Five, not three, most-mentioned *feelings* of the participating teachers were *anxiety, fearful, worried, overwhelmed,* and *sad*. These authorities are supporters of social-emotional learning (SEL), which is the process of developing the self-awareness, self-control, and interpersonal skills that are vital for schoolwork and life success.

Take a moment to think about what the participating teachers gave as their reasons for their emotions and feelings. Among the difficult problems reported by teachers during the pandemic have been caring for their own children and nonsupport from their administration while attempting to adapt to the new arrangements and program technologies for teaching by long-distance methods.

When schools reopened in some school districts, the six-feet distancing and masking requirements were implemented, but violations were evident in spite of efforts by the school personnel to comply with regulations. In any case, the pressures placed upon teachers today are reported to interfere with adequate rest/sleep and thus their teaching performance is reduced substantially.

IS THE TEACHER WORKLOAD TODAY MORE DEMANDING THAN IN EARLIER YEARS?

One might get a unanimous answer of "yes" to the title question above, but as it has been emphasized previously in this chapter, teacher load has been an ongoing problem in education historically. The following story of a "visiting teacher" much early in our history serves as a partial answer to the question of "increasing" teacher load. A large junior high school in the Lincoln, Nebraska School District, had what was called, "Scientist for Teacher Day." Highly experienced individuals in business and industrial position in the city would serve as a teacher for one full day while the teachers that they replaced took advantage of various professional development activities.

The visiting scientists did not teach the specific lessons that the regular teacher would have presented, but tied their lesson(s) to the purposes/knowledge/skills required in their professions and underscored the importance of gaining strong educational knowledge and skills for success in the field. One visiting scientist, Paul, was the chief engineer for the city's telephone and telegraph services. He was highly respected within the school community and earlier as a fighter airplane pilot in the U.S. air force.

After a full day of "teaching" students in five different classes, Paul was met at the classroom door by the chairman of the program. Both walked to the teachers' lounge for refreshments. As Paul entered the room, he took a deep breath and then "plunged" down on a couch and said, "For heaven's sake, do teachers do this every day?" Paul had experienced a "taste of the work" that teachers perform each day in the classroom, except that the additional teacher responsibilities and requirements were not required in his day's work.

WHAT THE RESEARCH COMMONLY FINDS REGARDING THE OUTCOMES OF HEAVY TEACHER WORKLOADS

The "volumes" of empirical research that have been published historically on teacher workload would surprise most people. A common finding of the published research is that the workload of school teachers has continually expanded. An important question centers on how the expanded workload has affected the teacher's quality of performance. The following teachers' comments help answer the foregoing question:

- Virtually all of the reports on teacher workload underscore its negative effect on one's ability to sleep.
- The increasing stress accompanies increasing workload that their work performance suffers; student learning is inhibited.
- The heavy workload along with ongoing change requirements results in higher levels of teacher turnover.
- Work-life balance is evidenced as one of the leading reasons why teachers' classroom performance has been affected negatively.
- Extended work requirements related to administrative standards and ongoing record keeping interfere with the teacher's planning time and takes away the time that the teacher had to "enjoy" his or her homelife.
- The lack of strong administrative leadership has been noted as a primary cause of job dissatisfaction. Organizational climate that inhibits individual initiative and collaborative work relationships serves to facilitate teacher stress, burnout, and departure from the profession.

The loss of personal creativity in lesson planning, the inability to determine one's own teaching priorities, the inability to use one's personal strengths as opposed to implementing required external standards, and following mandated external standards rather than using one's own creativity all result in losses on the part of quality education programs for America's children and youth. Classroom teachers have criticized mandated lessons for several reasons. As one teacher commented, how can the teacher meet the individual student's best interests and needs and yet implement required lesson plans at the same time.

HISTORICAL UPDATES CONCERNING THE PROBLEM OF TEACHER WORKLOAD

One of the major problems currently facing education in America today is that of teacher workload. The COVID-19 pandemic in America and throughout the world has inhibited educational progress to an extent that will only be determined as time goes on. The following information centers on what the professional teacher is saying relative to the educational practices being implemented during this time in history. The comments by the teachers in practice speak for themselves:

> Today, teachers are being asked to do even more. Redesign the learning experience overnight. Keep teaching your current classes. All while taking care of our own children, and fielding help requests from parents and students, 24-hours-a-day, 7 days-a-week. (Room to Discover, 10-21-20)
>
> Personally, for me, my stress level is higher now that it's been in teaching. Trying to manage the new teacher workload, manage my family at home, ensuring they're safe and I'm not bringing anything home to them (ie, such as the virus). (Weber, 10-25-2020)
>
> The workload was high before the pandemic, but now it is higher. (Riley, 10-7-2020)
>
> Some are talking about resigning and leaving education all together. (Vincent, 10-6-2020)
>
> The system and schedule in the current form is unsustainable. Left as is, we will see steady and rapid teacher burnout and frustration in an already stressful time. (Vincent, 10-6-2020)
>
> The closures have come with a massive increase for teachers at home. (Fernandez, 3-25-2020)
>
> I ask myself a lot of days how much longer can I do this. (O'Dowd & Hagan, 10-30-2020)
>
> While the daily in-person interactions with the students have been positive, teachers still feel the pressure of a higher workload and the stressors of navigating a pandemic. (Weber, 10-25-2020)

Solutions to the problem of teacher load, similar to the voting problems that faced America's 2020 presidential election, cannot be called at this point and time. Solutions for teacher load were not knocking at the doorstep before the virus pandemic. In chapter 1, the history of the workload problem for teachers has been discussed. It is clear that the problem of teacher workload, as being a major problem in education historically, has been for many decades. The current virus pandemic has added immensely to this problem.

Nevertheless, when things get back to normal, the problem of teacher load will still be with us. Chapter 2 examines the various ways that have been implemented to define, measure, and equalize teacher load in America's schools. If America's schools continue to close and open and then close once again, implementing a workload formula to measure it is highly unlikely. The variability of educational learning programs among the hundreds of schools in the United States at this time in history does not favor a method for determining fair and equitable workload statistics. Only the statistics of "required hours of schoolwork" per day or week might provide some insight to the workload of any one teacher.

THE DAMAGING COVID-19 PANDEMIC!

America does foster the great hope that the virus pandemic will be resolved and that American's schools will return with additional knowledge as to the most effective strategies for educating the nation's children and youth.

Nevertheless, at this time in history (November 11, 2020), the virus pandemic was expanding throughout the 50 states. Few Americans fully realize the damage that the COVID-19 pandemic has had on student learning. In the final section of this chapter, a report on its effects on education thus far is examined. However, the number of deaths being raged on the American population at this point and time due to the virus pandemic is one of the nation's most devastating occurrences on the country in its long history.

As of November 15, 2020, 249,331 deaths in the United States were attributed to the COVID-19 virus (read that number once again, 249,331 deaths *to date*). In World War II, 291,557 U.S. military personnel died in battle. The COVID-19 deaths in the United States by November 15, 2020, had reached a figure of 249,331; 42,226 less than the number of U.S. military deaths lost in World War II. With great misfortune, the death rate of the virus pandemic remains on the "upscale" at this time in America's history.

In chapter 2, an emphasis is placed on the strategies that have been and can continue to be implemented to assess teacher workload in normal school situation.

A CHAPTER 1 TRUE AND FALSE QUIZ

Directions: For each of the following statements, check them as to which statements are true and which statements are false. Check your quiz score at the end of the quiz.

1. Although the problem of teacher load has been apparent in education for many decades, little or no empirical or basic research has been centered on this topic. True___ or False___
2. The terms "teacher workload" and "class size" are synonymous. True___ or False___
3. The first effort to devise a teacher load formula for measuring teacher load was not set forth until 1973. True___ or False___
4. The concept of a teacher's institute for the "preparation" of teachers was not implemented until 1935 when Franklin Roosevelt was president of the United States. True___ or False___
5. Although several formulas for "measuring" teacher load have been developed, no such formula has been set forth for measuring teacher load at the elementary school level. True___ or False___
6. It has been demonstrated historically that the workloads of teachers commonly are fairly implemented in practice. True___ or False___
7. Best personnel practices would place the emphasis on a teacher candidate's GPA scores as opposed to other characteristics such as the candidate's personal goals and interests. True___ or False___
8. Although the virus pandemic was or has been troublesome for teachers, strangely enough the strategy of "distance learning" has lessened the pressures on teachers and provided them with increased time to collaborate on program matters. True___ or False___
9. The apparent of online learning has opened the door to new and viable strategies for improving the learning for students at all levels. True___ or False___
10. Fortunately, the studies of teacher workload have demonstrated that the matter of teacher workload continues to be a major problem. True___ or False___

ANSWERS TO THE QUIZ

1. The answer to statement #1, that little or no empirical or basic research has been directed to the topic of teacher workload, is "False." Although most of the research has used the quantitative survey methods, many individuals have been interested in the problem of teacher workload over the years. For example, one of the first efforts to "measure" teacher load was demonstrated by Almack and Bursch in 1931. Over the years, approximately 20 teacher load formulas have been set forth for measuring teacher load at the secondary school level.
2. The answer to statement #2, that "teacher load" and "class size" are used synonymously for educational purposes, is "False." The term "class size" refers to only one component of the total workload of the teacher. The factor

of teacher workload includes many other load components such as the number of classes taught, number of subject preparations, cooperative duties, the length of class periods, and others. The number of pupils taught is just one of the several components that makeup the workload of the teacher.

3. The answer to statement #3, that the first significant effort to devise a teacher workload formula was set forth in 1963, is "False." One of the very first teacher load formulas was established much earlier by Almack and Bursch in 1931.

4. The answer to statement #4, the first effort to fund teacher institutes was implemented by Franklin Roosevelt in 1935, is "False." Henry Barnard, then superintendent of public education in Connecticut, personally funded teacher institutes in the early 1840s that met for a period of three days to teach lessons on the basics, globes, and school keeping. The institute concept grew nationally and ultimately led to the establishment of two-year normal schools throughout the nation.

5. The answer to statement #5, that no such formula for measuring teacher load at the elementary school level has been set forth, is "False." Although several formulas for measuring the workload of secondary school teachers have been established, we know of only one formula, the Norton-Bria formula, that measures the workload of elementary school teachers. This formula differs from other formulas that measure secondary teacher workload in that it results in the number of hours worked by the teacher in completing any and all activities that include his or her teaching activities/responsibilities.

6. The answer to statement #6, that the workloads of teachers commonly are fairly implemented in practice, is "False." In fact, the Douglass Teacher Load Formula, that has been used nationally in hundreds of schools, has found "great" differences in the load index of teachers in any one school. In fact, some studies have found that some teachers are assigned workloads that are twice the size of others in the school. In addition, it is not unusual to find that teachers new to the school have the highest workload indices in the school.

7. The answer to statement #7, that worrying about a prospective teacher's personal interests and goals before hiring them is far less important than learning about their past successes, is "False." Some authorities have suggested that the school district's personnel strategies are faulty and need to be changed. That is, knowing about a candidate's future goals and objectives looms important relative to keeping them on the job in the school overtime. In fact, it is well-known that approximately 20% of the new teachers who come into a school district will leave that district after their first year of teaching. Teacher retention, along with teacher workload, is another major problem facing education in America's schools.

8. The answer to the statement #8, that the virus pandemic has actually served to lessen the pressures and increased the time that teachers have to meet and confer, is False. On the contrary, the strategies that have had to be employed for teaching students during the pandemic have commonly led to more problems for teachers. The accompanying pressures of virtual learning, most often, have led to frustration and "burnout" on the part of the teaching force. Evidence, to date, has shown that many teachers have decided to leave the teaching profession and preparation programs are finding fewer individuals entering their training programs.
9. The answer to statement #9, that the reopening of schools and online learning during the pandemic have been highly successful throughout the nation, is "False." Although the data on this question have been somewhat difficult to collect and assess, the problem of teacher workload has been highly troublesome for the most part. The workload and its related frustrations have been expressed by experienced teaching personnel specifically. Unfortunately, the frustrations of workload and its resulting negative effects on family responsibilities of teachers have been expressed by professional teachers nationally.
10. The answer to statement #10, that the matter of teacher workload continues to be among education's most troublesome problems, is "True." Professional teachers throughout the nation, who have given their best to continue a beneficial program of learning for students during the pandemic, also have expressed major concerns relative to the difficulties of trying to teach and their major concern about work and family responsibilities. In short, if indeed there is some solution to the matter of student learning during the difficult times of a virus pandemic, it has not taken place, to our knowledge, in America to date.

QUIZ SCORING RESULTS

10–8 correct: Very nice work
7–5 correct: Nice work
4–2 correct: Some good work shown
1–0 correct: Some work needed

KEY CHAPTER IDEAS AND RECOMMENDATIONS

- The primary factors that contribute to a teacher's workload have been identified. Class size is just one component of workload.

- A key point regarding teacher workload is vested in the fact that inequities of load commonly are evidenced when the newest and best teachers are carrying the highest workloads. When these teachers become so overly burdened, their efforts often are forced to a level of actual mediocrity.
- People leave positions for a variety of reasons. Low salary is important but is not the only reason. Workload and the inability to deal with required family responsibilities loom important. The COVID-19 pandemic has added greatly to the problems of teacher workload and teacher retention.
- The primary factors that contribute to teacher workload have been identified. The number of classes taught, the length of the class periods, the number of preparations, the nature of the subject being taught, including class size, constitute the primary factors that make up the total load weight index of the teacher.
- The COVID-19 pandemic has had a major impact on educational practices in general. Yet, student learning specifically leads the list of "losses" of most importance.
- Historically, the "solutions" for the problem of teacher workload have been based on inhibiting solutions rather than facilitating education practices. For example, reducing the curricular offerings in the school has been done to reduce the need for more teachers but has increased the class size numbers in other classes as a result.
- The knowledge of the nation's citizenry regarding teacher load has been faulty and misjudged. A common response to the matter of teacher load is that teachers only work nine months and have additional days off due to Spring break and multiple days off due to the many national holidays. However, an in-depth analysis of a teacher's workday and work-year tells the real story of the workload problem that teachers have encountered historically.
- *The need for assuring ongoing professional growth and development for all teaching personnel has been on the list of important priorities historically. In 1840, for example, the first teacher institutes were implemented by Henry Bernard. In 1840, Barnard used his personal funds to carry out the first teacher institute that included a three-day program of teaching the basics, globes, and the basics of education. This early "preparation" activity for teachers lead ultimately to the implementation of teacher institutes, normal schools, and colleges of education for teacher preparation.
- More than 20 teacher load formulas have been developed in America since 1931. In spite of this fact, few schools nationally have capitalized on these formulas in an attempt to equalize the workload of teachers in the nation's schools.
- *Survey studies of teacher workload over the years have revealed the many inequities that exist in the area of teacher workload in America's

schools. The COVID-19 pandemic has served to enhance the problems of education, in general, the major problem of teacher load specifically. Loss of teaching personnel and loss of student learning have been the unfortunate result.
- Gaining a better opportunity is one primary reason why people leave a position. Educational leaders must work diligently to find ways for people to advance within the field of education. Such advancement should not be to higher school positions only, rather new job responsibilities within a specific school itself must be explored and utilized. For example, a teacher of Grade 5 in an elementary school might be appointed as the school's reading resource teacher, school librarian, elementary school representative on the school district's curriculum committee, audio-visual/instructional resources coordinator, research disseminator for the school, newsletter editor, parent/teacher liaison, and other title positions with some necessary instructional purpose.
- The negative outcomes of teacher heavy workloads are inhibiting the quality of student learning, increasing the willingness of teachers to leave the profession, and decreasing the interest of young students to consider education as their career goal.

REFERENCES

Almack, J. C., & Bursch, J. F. (1925). *The Administration of Consolidated and Village Schools.* Houghton-Mifflin Co., New York, 1925.

Bloss, J. M. (1882). *Thirteenth Report of the Superintendent of Public Instruction of the State of Indiana to the Governor.* Indianapolis: State of Indiana.

Chisholm, L. L. (1953). *The Work of the Modern High School.* The MacMillan Company, New York, pp. 468–69.

Cipriano, C., & Brackett, M. (2020, April 7). Teachers are anxious and overwhelmed: They need SEL now more than ever before. *Currents ED Surge. Bainbridge Island Arts and Culture.* Bainbridge Island, WA. Ed Surge.

Davis, C. O. (1923). The Size of Classes and the Teaching Load in the High Schools Accredited the North Central Association. *School Review.*

Douglass, H. R. (1951). The 1950 revision of the Douglass high school teacher load formula. *NASSP Bulletin,* 35, 13–14.

Koos, F. H. (1922). The Load of the High School Teacher. *American School Board Journal.*

Norton, M. S. (1959). *Teacher Load in Nebraska High Schools in Cities From 5,000 to 25,000 Population.* Unpublished doctoral dissertation. Department of Educational Administration & Supervision, University of Nebraska-Lincoln.

Norton, M. S., & Bria, R. (1992). Toward an equitable measure of elementary school teacher load. *Record in Educational Administration and Supervision,* 13(1), 62–66.

Room to Discover (2020, October 21). *Managing teacher workload: How to Do More in Less Time.* From the web: https://roomtodiscoverl.com/teacher-workload/

Santry, C. (2019, October 15). Teachers May Quit. From the Web: https://www.tes.com/new/quarter-teachers-may-quit-mainly-due-workload.

Stroud, G. (2016, October 8). The frustrating moment when I knew I had to give up on teaching. From the web: http: //www.amamamia.com.au/gabbie-stroud-teacher/

Chapter 2

Calculating and Assessing the Workload of Teacher Personnel

Primary chapter goal: To discuss the primary formulas for measuring teacher load and how the results of workload assessments can serve to gain equity among members of the school's faculty.

Chapter 1 identified several teacher workload formulas that have been set forth over the past several decades. The identified formulas have differed primarily by the work components that were utilized in "measuring" the teachers' workloads. Over time, the Douglass Teacher Load Formula has been the most recognized and utilized formula for determining teacher load at the secondary school level. The Norton/Bria teacher load formula is the one formula that is utilized for determining teacher load at the elementary school level.

One thing seems certain. The problems surrounding teacher workload cannot be resolved unless we do something positive about it. The need to resolve the inequities that exist among teaching faculty members is one matter that must be addressed. A second need is that of the importance of applying the knowledge that we do have on hand to assess and evaluate the status of teacher workload within the schools. It seems clear that the present conditions of the COVID-19 pandemic inhibit "solutions" that might apply during normal times. It is clear that attempts to initiate virtual means for student learning have their own problems. To date, "homeschooling" has not been effective for all students.

WHY THE DETERMINATION OF TEACHER LOAD IS SO IMPORTANT IN SCHOOL SETTINGS

Chapter 1 identified several problems related to teacher workload in the public schools of America. First and foremost is the evidence of major inequities in the workload of teacher personnel among the nation's schools. In some cases, some teachers have been reported as having a load index twice that of other teachers in the same school. The negative outcomes of such situations are shown by the loss of teacher personnel in education—by "burnout" that reduces the effectiveness of some of the best teachers in the school system and a decreasing interest on the part of some individuals for entering the education profession.

It is quite clear that the results of inequitable workload assignments are not fully understood by school leaders or by the teachers themselves. For example, studies have revealed the fact that some teachers with the lowest workload indices are under the impression that they are carrying "too high a workload." In most cases, these teachers are carrying the lowest workload indices of all the teaching staff (Norton, 1959). Attempts to "inform" a teacher that he or she is carrying a lighter load than most all of the other teachers on the faculty fall short of being convincing. Some specific evidence of this fact becomes necessary. It is at this point that a fair and equitable teacher load formula comes into play.

A LIGHTBULB EXPERIENCE

It is of interest, and of considerable importance, to keep in mind that teachers, like all human beings, do differ. So what? In an early study by Norton (1959), it was found that many teachers, who actually were carrying the lightest workload according to the Douglas Teacher Load Formula, were of the opinion that they were carrying the highest workloads in their schools. Such research findings are of importance since actual statistics, determined by reliable research sources, can serve to help such teachers understand that their workload is not among the greatest ones in the school.

On one occasion, the band/orchestra teacher in one high school was asked about initiating a beginning band program in the school. The teacher, of course, was not only surprised but insisted that his workload was already overburdened. When the high school principal shared the teacher's workload results based on the Douglass Teacher Load Formula, he was overly surprised that his load was below the average workload of other teachers in the school.

In fact, the teacher's school workload was among the lowest in the school. His workload was self-imposed by his "outside-the-school" orchestra activities in which he participated and most often received compensation. In short, he was creating his own workload primarily by taking on outside program assignments, some without and some with personal compensation. The teacher intelligently recognized that his overload was an outcome of his own making. He was personally convinced that his outside-the-school program activities had to be substantially reduced.

THE LONG ROAD TRAVELED IN SEARCH OF A VALID TEACHER LOAD FORMULA

It is interesting to note that Douglass's interest in measuring teacher load objectively covered a span of over three decades. In 1928, he developed a formula to measure teacher load at the secondary school level. He was aware of the tendency to assign teachers the responsibility for five class periods. However, he showed a concern for the fact that teachers also were carrying extracurricular activities such as dramatics, the glee club, the school orchestra, the school newspaper, the school yearbook, club activities, the study hall duty, after-school student activities, school office/administrative chores, and other such works. Time for teacher classroom preparation and study was minimal.

Although the increase of class time from 50 minutes to 55 minutes does not seem like a major change, it did add 25 new minutes to the instructional time of the teachers. Additional instructional time adds to the time needed in preparation time requirements as well. In view of these factors, Douglass felt that carefully worked out lesson plans were out of the question and that the strain of teaching was such that it was unwise for any teacher to spend more than nine hours a day at work and for the majority of teachers eight hours should be the rule.

All of the foregoing "discussion" led toward the question of "what was fair." In the absence of a better formula, Douglass suggested the following:

$$\text{Total pupils} - (\text{no. of classes} \times 25) \qquad 60$$

The 25 in the formula was selected on the assumption that 25 was close to the optimum size of a high school class. At that time, it was the standard set by the North Central Association of Secondary Schools and Colleges. This formula included only two variables, the number of classes and number of pupils. It was recognized that teaching load is made up of other variables such as the number of class preparations required in the various subjects and the length of the class periods. Douglass proposed that the most significant of these components at the time was the number of required preparations. He stated that "perhaps it is fair to say, in the absence of any more reliable data, that with the respect to this teaching load three preparations are approximately equal to a class recitation plus preparation" (Douglass, 1928, p. 23). So, as a result, Douglass added the following to the foregoing early formula:

$$\frac{\text{Total pupils} - (\text{No. of classes} \times 25)}{60} + \frac{\text{prep.} - 3}{3}$$

A key note at this point is the concern of Douglass for the differences that might exist when teaching the various subjects. That is, should the teaching of a subject in science receive more weight than another subject such as social studies? This concern led to the study of all of the "work" that is required by teaching the various subjects. Douglass wisely pointed out that if the matter of providing standards for judging and equating teaching load were to be carried further it would be necessary to work out coefficients by which the teaching load for different subjects might be equated.

Such thinking led the study of the work requirements necessary for teaching a subject. The result was the revolutionary Subject Grade Coefficient (SGC). Table 2.1 sets forth the SGC rating for the 13 subjects being taught in the schools at this early time. The SGC is a multiplicative factor, so multiplication by the number 1 does not increase the value of any figure (e.g., 1 × 17 = 17). However, 1.1 × 17 = 18.7. In the same way, an SGC of .9 is less than one and it would decrease the number being multiplied (e.g., .9 × 17 = 15.3). The point here is that the SGC of the subject would either increase, decrease, or have no effect on the number serving as the multiplicand.

Keep in mind that the figures in Table 2.1 were established several years ago. Although the contemporary SGC figures have not been reestablished to our knowledge, table 2.1 serves the purposes set forth for chapter 2.

Table 2.1 Average Number of Minutes Spent Daily Per Class Period at Various Levels in Various Subject Areas and Derived Subject Grade Coefficients

Subject	Grade 9	Grades 10-11-12	Coefficients for Grades 9	10-11-12
English	90	94	1.1	1.1
Art	74	84	.9	1.0
Home Economics	81	90	1.0	1.1
Music	85	82	1.0	1.0
Mathematics	80	83	1.0	1.0
Agriculture	-----	109	-----	1.3
Industrial Arts	79	83	.9	.9
Physical Ed.	73	80	.9	.9
Commercial	82	80	1.0	1.0
Social Studies	89	96	1.1	1.1
Foreign Lang.	90	85	1.0	1.0
Science	105	93	1.1	1.1
Health	----	105	1.1	1.2

THE 1950 VERSION OF THE 1950 DOUGLASS TEACHER LOAD FORMULA: GETTING DOWN TO BUSINESS

The foregoing information that accrued over many years resulted in the 1950 version of the Douglass Secondary Teacher Load Formula that has been available to school leaders since that time. Teachers have continued to complain about their workload and school administrators have pleaded for more funds to increase teachers' compensation and hire additional faculty personnel, but little has been done to demonstrate teacher load inequities since the formula was established. In the following sections of the chapter, the specific Douglass formula is set forth and examples of its application in practice are presented.

Although, overtime, the formula has been implemented in various school districts in the nation, its application in school practices has not been demonstrated by formal adoption of school policy by local school boards. The reason for this absence is vested in the fact that few school leaders have knowledge of the Douglass formula and faculty personnel in administrator preparation programs are equally "ignorant" of the formula's benefits. They seem to understand the singular term of "class size."

THE BOOK'S STUDY SECTION

The foregoing *criticism* underscores the primary purposes of why this book was written. A wide understanding of the strategies for assessing and evaluating teacher workload in the nation's schools would result in major improvements in teacher retention and intern on student learning. The following section of the book is termed as a "study" section. That is, just reading the section might be somewhat informative, but a study of the information presented is necessary for gaining an effective understanding.

Specific applications of the Douglass and Norton/Bria teacher load formulas are presented. The "reader" should take time to examine each example by working through each step of an example workload problem.

The Douglass Teacher Load Formula is as follows:

$$TL = SGC\,[(CP - DUP/10) + (NP - 25\,CP)/100]\,[(PL + 50/100]$$

$$+\,0.6\,PC\,[(PL + 50)/100]$$

Where:

TL = Units of teaching load per week.
SGC = Subject Grade Coefficient.
CP = Class periods spent in the classroom per week.
DUP Factor = Number of class periods spent per week in classroom; teaching classes for which the preparation is very similar to that for some other section, not including the original section.
NP = Number of pupils per week.
PL = Gross length of class periods in minutes.
PC = Number of class periods spent per week in supervision of study halls, homeroom, students' activities, teacher's meetings, committee work, and other noninstructional activities.

STEPS FOR CALCULATING THE ACTUAL TEACHER LOAD

The following major section of chapter 2 centers on the calculation and application of the Douglass formula. Once again, we focus on this formula because of its long history of development and its effective application in school districts nationally. The key purpose is straightforward: If you study the formula and understand it, it is an accomplishment that you can implement in education and one that you can "teach" others who will benefit as well.

The following section is a *study section* and reading alone will not be satisfactory for gaining a clear understanding of how to apply the Douglass formula in practice. We suggest that you read through the following section and return later for taking the time needed for the best understanding of the formula's calculations.

The steps for implementing the Douglass formula are as follows:

Step 1: Obtain the following data for each teacher in the school.
    A. For each section taught.
        a. the length of the class period
        b. the name of the subject
        c. the grade level (secondary) of majority of students in the section
        d. the number of students in the section
        e. whether the class is or is not a duplicate section—remember, of two similar sections, one is an original and the other is a duplicate.
        f. the number of periods per week the class meets.
    B. The number of minutes spent legitimately weekly on the average throughout the semester in all school duties other than teaching classes.

Step 2: Treating separately each class section or group of similar class sections (e.g., three first-year algebra sections), compute the load incident to that section or group of sections not using the term (0.6 PC [(PL + 50)/100]). Be sure to substitute the following: SGC, CP, DUP., NP, and PL. DUP is 0 for all original sections. Get appropriate SGC from table values.

Step 3: Divide the total number of minutes per week on the average of all other school duties by 84 (one decimal place only, to get PC). Substitute that number for PC in the last term of the formula.

Step 4: Now add the load figures for each class section and the load figures for nonteaching duties. The result is the number of teaching load units for the given teacher.

AN EXAMPLE OF ONE SOCIAL STUDY TEACHER'S WORKLOAD

Example #1

The social studies teacher has the following classes:
  1 class of World History with 28 students, Grade 10;
  1 class of Problems of American Democracy with 27 students, Grade 12;
  1 class of American History with 26 students, Grade 11;
  2 classes of English with 28 and 31 students, Grade 12

Six periods a week for nine weeks in the semester coaching a debate squad is equivalent of three class periods for the semester. Two class periods on average through the semester on committee work and other cooperatives. Class period length is 55 minutes.

Computation of the Workload:

$$TL = 1.1[25 - 5/10 + (700 - 625)/100)[55 + 50]/100]$$
$$+ 0.6 \times 5[55 + 50]/100] = 1.1 \times 25.25 \times 1.05 + 3.15 = 32.31$$

(This teacher s load is slightly above the median standard.)

Example #2 (Use the Douglass Teacher Load Formula)

The science/math teacher has the following classes:
  2 classes of physics with 2 double periods with 24 and 26 pupils, Grade 11.
  3 classes of algebra with 26, 24, and 29 pupils, Grade 10.
  3 hours (4 class periods) a week on the average spent in cooperations.

Class periods are 45 minutes in length.

Computation of the Workload:

$$\text{Physics load} = 1.1[(14 - 9/10) + (350 - 350)/100][(45 + 50/100)]$$

$$= 1.1(14 - 9/10)(.95) = 13.69$$

$$\text{Algebra load} = 1.0[(15 - 10/10) + (390 - 375)/100][(45 + 50/100)]$$

$$= 1(15 - 10/10) + 15(.95) = 13.44$$

$$\text{Cooperations} - .6 \times 4[(45 + 50/100)] = 2.28$$

$$\text{Total Load} = 13.69 + 13.44 + 2.28 = 29.41$$

(This teacher's load is at the median standard.)

Example #3

A high school science teacher has five classes of biology each day. Class periods are 50 minutes in length. Pupil class enrollments are 28, 31, 23, 28, and 27. During the semester, the teacher averages the equivalent of four class periods per week in cooperative assignments. The SGC for high school science is 1.1.

Step 1: Determine the values for the variables in the Douglass formula.
SGC = 1.1 for 10th grade science.
CP = 25 (Teacher has 5 daily classes and each meets 5 times a week.)
DUP = 20 (Teacher has 4 duplicate preparations 5 times per week. Thus, 4 × 5 = 20.)
NP = 28 + 31 + 23 + 28 + 27 = 137 each day. 137 × 5 days per week = 685.
PL = 50 minutes.
PC = 4 class periods equivalency per week.

Step 2: Substitute values and perform calculations.
TL = 1.1 [(25 − 20)/10 + (685 − 25[25])/100] [(50 + 50)/100 + 0.6 (4) [(50 + 50)/100] = 28.6 (This teacher's load is just between the low and median standard score.)

THE REVISED NORMS FOR HIGH SCHOOL TEACHING LOAD

Table 2.2 shows the revised norms for high school teaching loads for twelve specific subjects, one mixed load, and the average load for all subjects. For example, the teaching load norms for social studies is 26.7 for the lower quartile, 30.3 for the median load, and 33.8 for the upper quartile rating. Thus, the English

Table 2.2 Revised Norms for High School Teaching Load

Subject	Lower Q.	Md.	Upper Q.
English	27.5	30.7	36.8
Social Studies	26.7	30.3	33.8
Mathematics	25.4	29.6	34.1
Commercial	25.5	28.5	31.3
Science	25.4	30.4	34.0
Home Economics	26.5	29.4	32.2
Industrial Arts	25.4	28.2	31.4
Vocational Ag.	30.8	33.6	36.6
Foreign Language	26.4	28.3	30.2
Physical Education	27.6	30.3	35.0
Music	26.7	29.6	31.2
Art	25.4	29.3	32.5
Mixed Loads	29.1	31.3	33.7
All Subjects	27.3	29.9	32.9

teacher's load established in the foregoing example (32.31) would fall above the median rating of 30.7. The math/science teacher's score of 29.41 would be rated as being in the lower quartile for mixed load teachers (see Table 2.2).

THE NORTON/BRIA TEACHER WORKLOAD FORMULA FOR GRADES 1 TO 6 SCHOOL TEACHERS

The Norton/Bria teacher load formula differs from the Douglass formula in that it focuses on the number of hours the teacher works opposed to resulting in a workload index. Nevertheless, the final formula calculation of the teacher's workload in hours can be compared to the "expected work hours" for workers in the school along with checking the equity among the workload of teachers within the school and school system. Such responsibilities fall at the office door of the school principal. Most commonly, the school principal is the individual who determines teacher instructional assignments and cooperative duties of teachers.

The Norton/Bria teacher workload formula is written as follows (Norton, 1992):

TLH = 3/2 ATH + (SL × PH)/CM + F' or F" (OG × PH + 0.6 [CH])
where TLH = Assigned teaching hours of time per week.
ATH = Assigned teaching hours in the classroom per week.
SL = Actual number of students taught above or below the average class size for any given grade (class size can be altered according to local or state class size norms).

PH = Preparation hours (one-half the actual time for assigned hours in the classroom per week: 1/2 ATH).
CM = Standard class mean size.
F' = 1/16 (use for small- and medium-sized school districts).
F'' = 1/13 (use for larger school districts).
OG = Other grades taught in a single classroom under the direction of one teacher (e.g., for a teacher who teaches Grades 2 and 3 simultaneously in one room, OG = 1).
CH = Cooperative hours spent in noninstructional duties such as meetings, playground supervision, parental conferences, and other nonteaching assignments.

PUTTING THE NORTON/BRIA WORKLOAD FORMULA TO WORK

Example #1

Elaine Ora teaches at the Lafayette Elementary School that has a total school enrollment of 224 students. Miss Ora's sixth-grade class has an enrollment of 32 students. Her teaching day begins at 8:30 a.m. and ends at 2:45 p.m. She has a 30-minute lunch break and supervises two recess periods each which last for 20 minutes. Other related school duties include faculty meetings, parental conferences, after-school club activities, and attending district-level meetings for a total co-op time of 11 hours and 15 minutes weekly.

LOAD CALCULATION

ATH = 25 hr. 25 min. (Teaching hours per week are 5 days multiplied by 6 hr. and 15 min. per day less 5 days × 40 min. each day for recess and 5 days × 30 min. each day for lunch. (PH = ½ ATH = ½ (25 hr. 25 min. =12 hr. 43 min.

SL = 7 [Student load is based on the actual number of students above or below the average class size for Grade 3. It is calculated as a fractional measure of the time needed for preparation. The average class size for Grade 3 is 25 as shown in the chart below.

$$7 \times (12 \text{ hr. } 43 \text{ min.})/25 = 3 \text{ hr. } 34 \text{ min.}$$

TABLE FOR AVERAGE CLASS SIZE

Grade 1	24 students
Grade 2	25 students
Grade 3	24 students
Grade 4	27 students
Grade 5	28 students
Grade 6	28 students

CM = 25; OG = 0 (no extra grades taught); F' = 1/16; CH= 6 hr. 45 min. (0.6 × 675 min./week) = 405 min./week = 6 hr. 45 min.

Substituting into the formula and rounding any fractional minutes to the nearest whole minute:

$$TLH = 3/2(25 \text{ hr. } 25 \text{ min.}) + (7 \times 12 \text{ hr. } 43 \text{ min.})/25$$

$$+ 1/16(0 \times 12 \text{ hr. } 43 \text{ min.}) + 6 \text{ hr } 45 \text{ min.}$$

$$= 38 \text{ hr. } 8 \text{ min.} + 3 \text{ hr. } 34 \text{ min.} + 0 + 6 \text{ hr. } 45 \text{ min.}$$

$$= \textbf{48 hr. 27 min. per week}$$

Example #2: The Norton/Bria Formula

An elementary school teacher has 16 fifth grade students and 14 sixth grade students in 1 classroom in a medium-sized school district. Classes begin at 8:45 a.m. and end at 3:15 p.m. Recesses are for 25 minutes, once in the morning and once in the afternoon. Lunch period for the teacher is 30 minutes. Other cooperatives include faculty meetings, 60 minutes per week; 30 minutes per day coaching intramurals, 180 minutes per week; and parental conferences, 30 minutes per week.

Step 1: Determine the values of the time components for the Norton/Bria formula.

ATH = 25 hr. 50 min. (6 hr. 30 min. per day × 5 days per week - 5 × 80 min. (recesses and lunch time)) = 25 hr. 50 min.

SL = 2 (standard class size for grades 5 and 6 is 28. Student load is based on the actual number of students [30] less the average standard class size [28] = 2).

CM = 28 (standard class size mean is 28).

OG = 1 (one grade other than Grade 5 is taught in the same classroom.).

F' = 1/16 (medium-sized school district).
CH = 5 hr. (faculty meetings, 60 min.; district meetings, 30 min.; intramurals, 180 min.;
and parental conferences, 30 min. = 300 min. or 5 hr.)

Step 2: Substitute values in the Norton/Bria formula and calculate.

$$TLH = 3/2\left(25 \text{ hr. } 50 \text{ min.}\right) + \left(2 \times 12 \text{ hr. } 55 \text{ min.}\right)/28$$

$$+ 1/6\left(1 \times 2 \text{ hr. } 55 \text{ min.}\right) + .6\left(5 \text{ hr.}\right)$$

$$38 \text{ hr. } 45 \text{ min.} + 55 \text{ min.} + 48 \text{ min.} + 3 \text{ hr.} = 43.5 \text{ hr.}$$

A CONCLUSION

Once that a load formula is programmed, computer technology is put to work. The calculation of the teacher load is reduced to the insertion of the load data required in the formula. The use of computer technology completes the task of computing the data. A 40–hour workweek has been viewed as the typical workweek in America. Time spent over 40 hours has been termed "overtime" and extra compensation is given to the worker. In education positions, payment for overtime is not a common practice; but it is a common expectation.

AN EXAMINATION OF THE TEACHER LOAD IN 17 DIFFERENT SCHOOL DISTRICTS IN ONE STATE

The determination of the teacher load in school districts nationally, although of some interest, was beyond the scope of this book. Nevertheless, illustrating the similarities and differences of teacher load statistics within one state was viewed as meeting the book's major purposes. Thus, the following section centers on the discussion of secondary school teacher load in 17 different cities in one state with populations from 5,000 to 25,000 people.

The contention that some school districts have schools whereby teacher loads differ widely has been noted previously. That is, one teacher in the same school might have a teacher load index twice that of a teacher with the lowest index. Can this contention be verified? The answer to that question is answered in the following section. The populations of the 17 cities and their school districts' statistics are as shown in Table 2.3.

Table 2.3 School Districts' Secondary Teacher Load Statistics

Subject	Q_1	Md.	Q_3
English	28.4	31.2	33.3
Science	28.1	30.7	33.0
Agriculture	24.4	27.8	32.4
Mathematics	27.3	30.2	32.3
Commercial/Business	27.2	30.0	32.2
Foreign Language	27.6	29.3	31.8
Social Studies	29.1	31.3	31.3
Industrial Arts	24.1	26.4	30.3
Home Economics	23.7	25.3	28.4
Music	16.8	19.8	25.7
Physical Education	17.5	21.0	25.4
All Subjects	25.5	29.2	32.0

TEACHER LOAD AVERAGES COMPARED WITH TEACHING EXPERIENCE

Although just one study of teacher load cannot be viewed as being applicable to all school districts in all the states, one study of teacher load averages compared to teaching experience was completed in one state; 363 secondary school teachers were included in the study. Table 2.4 sets forth the teachers' experience by years, the number of teachers at the six levels of experience, the average teaching load for each level of experience, the average cooperative load for each of the years of experience, and the average total teacher load for the participants.

As shown in Table 2.4 and as indicated in this one study, teachers in their first year of teaching had the second highest average teaching load of the entire teaching group. This finding gives some credibility to the oft-heard statement that teachers new to teaching commonly carry the greater teaching loads. In fact, as shown in the average teaching load column of Table 2.4, first-year teachers do indeed have the highest teacher load index; their cooperative load average index slightly lowers their total index score. Of some interest is the finding that the "oldest" teachers in the group of 363 teachers had the lowest teaching and lowest cooperative load indices.

TAKE OVER FOR ONE DAY AS SCHOOL PRINCIPAL

Assume that you are the school principal at Lafayette High School. Your foreign language teacher comes to you with a request to drop one class of Spanish next semester since the first-semester load is much too high. You have calculated

Table 2.4 Teacher Load Average Compared to Teaching Experience

Experience	# of Teachers	Aver. Teaching Load	Aver. Coop. Load	Total Aver. Load
No Exper.	30	25.39	7.27	32.66
1-4 years	84	24.78	7.98	32.76
5-9 years	84	23.91	7.09	31.00
10-19 years	67	24.73	8.03	32.76
20-29 years	55	23.84	7.96	31.80
30 + years	42	23.71	6.55	30.26

the teacher's load index for the current semester and it is 34. 2. For the first semester, the teacher has 3 classes of Spanish 1 with 17, 19, and 15 students; 1 class of Spanish 2 with 22 students; and 1 class of English with 25 students.

As cooperative duties, the teacher serves as the coach for the girls' volleyball team and serves as a coeditor of the school's student newspaper. What response might you have in mind for this teacher's request to lower the workload by cutting one class subject in the second semester?

Evidence: The foreign language teacher's first-semester workload index is 34.2. This figure is above the 3rd quartile rating for the school district's foreign language teachers' index as a whole; it is 31.8. In addition, the teacher's load index of 34.2 is above that of the average load index for all school teachers. That index is 32.0. It does appear that some adjustment in the foreign language teacher's workload is in order. However, the first semester will be completed in six weeks. Which option, among the following, might you choose?

Choice #1—Leave the work assignment as is for now. The first semester ends in six weeks and things could be different.

Choice #2—Tell the teacher that you will check with personnel office to see if "extra pay" is possible in this case.

Choice #3—Ask the teacher if only two classes of Spanish 1 would suffice for the second semester. The two remaining classes could incorporate the additional students.

Choice #4—See if the teacher could reevaluate the cooperative duties. For example, could the teacher drop or reduce any of the current extra cooperative duties.

Choice #5—Ask about having a student serve as the teacher's student helper (intern) who is assigned various responsibilities as fits the case.

Choice # 6—None of the above. However, here is the decision/action that I would take:

Note: If this "in-basket" matter is considered in a graduate class of students, divide the students in the class into appropriate small groups and give each group a specific time to consider a recommendation for "resolving" the foregoing matter. Have each group report their administrative recommendations in a feedback session.

The factors that make up a teacher's workload have been identified in the Douglass and Norton/Bria workload formulas. However, there are many other *conditions* that affect teaching as well. Most all such conditions tend to add or reduce the workload of the teacher. Schools without a full-time principal, teaching in classrooms with excessively noisy surroundings, inadequate clerical help, and inadequate instructional resource materials are examples of conditions that affect teaching in a negative way.

Following are examples of *school conditions* that tend to affect workload in a negative way:

- Textbooks and supplies not adequate: 30 of 61 teachers said this made the workload heavier.
- Extra duties assigned to you not of the type you prefer: 36 of 74 teachers said this made the workload heavier.
- General feeling among teachers that a sincere effort is not being made to distribute the teaching, load fairly: 21 of 68 teachers said that this made the workload heavier.
- The majority of your students are not appreciative or responsive: 30 of 44 teachers said that this made the workload heavier.
- Unsatisfactory or inadequate clerical in school office: 21 of 57 teachers said that this made the workload heavier.
- You do not have a desk at school for your own exclusive use: 30 of 68 teachers said that this made the workload heavier.
- Principal with real insight into problems faced by teachers not present: 24 of 56 teachers said this made the workload heavier.
- School library services not available: 8 of 13 teachers said this made the workload heavier.
- Special problems in your classroom due to numbers of handicapped or unresponsible pupils: 49 of 91 teachers said that this made the workload heavier.
- Forward looking, professionally minded principal not present: 12 of 36 teachers said this made the workload heavier.

Following are examples of *curriculum and facility conditions* that affect teacher workload:

- Curricular experiments affecting the teacher's classes: 18 of 37 teachers said this made the workload heavier.

- Class sessions frequently interrupted by bulletins, announcements, errands, or special events: 50 of 135 of teachers said that this made the workload heavier.
- School as a whole excessively overcrowded: 56 or 133 teachers said that this made the workload heavier.
- Excessively noisy classrooms: 13 of 42 teachers said this makes the workload heavier.
- Inadequate workroom facilities for classroom teachers: 46 of 143 teachers said this made the workload heavier.
- Inadequate restroom facilities for classroom teachers: 25 of 42 teachers said that this made the workload heavier.
- Inadequate or unsatisfactory custodial services: 14 of 33 teachers said this makes the workload heavier.
- Other conditions that affect teacher load: 28 of 34 teachers said this makes the workload heavier.

WORKLOAD RESPONSES FROM INDIVIDUAL TEACHERS OF VARIOUS SUBJECTS

Secondary teachers were asked about conditions/factors that affected their subject specialty. That is, were there conditions/factors that were directly related to the subject(s) they were teaching.

Their responses were somewhat overwhelming. A few examples of the teachers' responses are mentioned to illustrate this "special" kind of teacher load problem.

English teacher: "No teacher should be expected to teach 92 pupils 'theme writing' and be able to do justice to the pupils."

Commerce teacher: "Not enough business machines to teach adequately an office training course."

Industrial Arts teacher: "Not enough equipment."

English teacher: "Uneven loads and unfair salaries."

Commerce teacher: "Lack of time for individual help before and after school due to committee meetings and so forth."

Foreign Language teacher: "Heterogenous classes make my load heavier."

Music teacher: "Need more help for individual and small group work."

Physical Education teacher: "Crowded conditions makes it necessary for me to teach all my classes in a different room."

Physical Education teacher: "Curriculum changes without contacting teachers affected."

Music teacher: "Sponsoring singing groups for service clubs, church groups and so forth."

TEACHER WORKLOAD IS DETERMINED BY THE NUMBER OF PUPILS A TEACHER HAS IN THE CLASSROOM: OR IS IT?

Of course, the answer to the above title question is "yes" in part. In one state study, the participants did contend that their workload is a major source of pressure for them. However, other conditions that add to the teacher's workload, and load factors that have not been specifically mentioned previously, are noted here.

The statistics are reported for men and women teachers separately. Percent figures represent the statistics for those that replied in the study that the condition was a factor of *considerable strain/pressure* for them. That is, in the first entry related to planning and class preparation, 38% of the men teachers viewed the requirements of instructional planning and class preparation as causing considerable strain for them.

Workload due to the requirements of instructional planning and class preparation: (men—38%) (women—42%)
Workload due to the changing emphasis in classroom methods and procedures: (men—38%) (women—38%)
Workload due to clerical and administrative work: (men—38%) (women—38%)
Workload due to guidance and pupil-adjustment responsibilities: (men—38%) (women—38%)
Workload due to required community relationships: (men—38%) (women—41%)
Workload due to professional improvement requirements: (men—38%) (women—42%)

The foregoing information/data related to factors of teacher workload are of paramount importance for several reasons. For example, teacher workload goes far beyond the factor of class size. In addition, it is clear that teacher workload goes beyond the factors considered in the calculation of load by load formulas such as the Douglass Teacher Load Formula and the Norton/Bria formula. Climate and condition factors that are not specifically considered in such "mathematical" formulas certainly do exist and affect workload results for personnel commonly in different ways.

School conditions affected by a school district's policy mandates, the relations of school teachers/parents, and the school climate in general are

TEACHERS' THOUGHTS ABOUT THEIR OWN WORKLOADS

The final table for chapter 2 centers on teachers' opinions about their own workloads. That is, what is the estimate of the teacher's strain relative to their workload and also their evaluation as to the weight of the workload from being reasonable, heavy, or extra heavy. For example, might a teacher with a low Douglass index of 20 or below think that their load was heavy? Table 2.5 reveals an answer to that question. As indicated in Table 2.5, eight teachers with load indices between 20 and 24 viewed their loads have been causing considerable strain. In addition, 29 and 9 teachers with low workloads of 20 to 24 considered their loads to be heavy or extra heavy.

In the same study, nine teachers with load indices of 40 to 44, which are quite heavy, rated their workloads as being reasonable. Two teachers, with the heaviest workloads of 45 units and above, viewed these loads as having little strain and also being reasonable. The information, set forth in Table 2.5, demonstrates several problems relative to "attempting" to gain some equality in assigning workloads to teachers. Teachers with the lightest load indices of load, in many cases, view the load as being of considerable strain. In addition, some of the same teachers consider their workload as being heavy or even extra heavy. Of course, related school conditions/climates most likely come into play in such cases. The concept of school climate is discussed in-depth in chapter 3.

Table 2.5 Teacher Load and the Evaluation of Strain and the Estimate of Load Index as Set Forth by Practicing Teachers. Table numbers represent teachers

Teacher Load Units	Source of Strain		Estimate of Workload			
	Little	Considerable	Light	Reasonable	Heavy	Extra Heavy
45-above	2	12	0	2	6	6
40-44	12	8	0	9	9	2
35-39	21	26	0	20	20	7
30-34	82	47	0	54	67	9
25-29	78	41	1	86	29	5
20-24	21	8	1	86	29	5
15-19	1	0	1	0	0	0

CHAPTER 2 QUIZ

Directions: Circle the correct answer in each of the following multiple-choice questions. Check your answers at the end of the questions posed.

1. When the "evidence" regarding teacher workload is clearly understood,
   (a) it is revealed that teacher workload varies widely in secondary schools.
   (b) it is revealed that teacher workload is an "emotional" characteristic as opposed to a factual condition.
   (c) it is demonstrated that teacher load cannot be determined by statistical data.
   (d) it can be used to compare workloads and identify inequities in teacher assignments.
   (e) none of the above.
2. The application of teacher workload formulas, such as the Douglass formula,
   a. has been the principal tool used by most every school in the nation for equalizing teacher workloads.
   b. can be used to explain teacher workloads to faculty personnel.
   c. has demonstrated, once and for all, that class size is the most important consideration in determining teacher workload.
   d. can be beneficial for the administrative personnel for determining teacher performance compensation.
   e. none of the above.
3. Teacher with the lower (20-24 indices) workloads, according to basic research studies, are likely to view the load as being
   a. heavy 75% of the time.
   b. unreasonable 75% of the time.
   c. reasonable 75% of the time.
   d. light 75% of the time.
   e. none of the above.
4. The SGC in the Douglass Teacher Load Formula stands for
   a. school graduation completions.
   b. standard group classes.
   c. subject grade coefficient.
   d. student grade and class.
   e. none of the above.
5. A primary reason for calculating the teachers' workloads is to
   a. check on their assigned responsibilities.
   b. determine performance salary.

c. to evaluate teacher performance.
d. to determine the equity of teacher workloads.
e. none of the above.
6. Which factor is not a component of the Douglass Teacher Load Formula?
   a. number of pupils being taught.
   b. class periods spent in the classroom per week.
   c. length of class periods.
   d. grouping of student academic abilities.
   e. cooperative duties assigned.
   f. none of the above.
7. The Norton/Bria teacher load formula
   a. measures the workload of secondary teachers whose subjects are required.
   b. measures the number of hours that an elementary school teacher works each week.
   c. measures the number of hours secondary teachers work each week.
   d. measures the index weight of each teacher for comparison purposes.
   e. none of the above.
8. Statistics related to teacher workload have been calculated for the following reasons:
   a. to determine the workload indexes for beginning and experienced teachers.
   b. to determine the workloads of teachers in different subject areas.
   c. to determine the cooperative workloads of secondary school teachers with different years of experience.
   d. to determine the opinions of practicing teachers are to the "strain/weight" of their teacher load.
   e. all of the above.
   f. none of the above.
9. Which characteristic(s) below is/are *not measured* in either the Douglass or Norton/Bria teacher load formulas:
   a. teacher's emotions regarding the teacher's workload.
   b. teacher's concept of job satisfaction.
   c. teacher's cooperative duties.
   d. teacher's hours worked during one week.
   e. all of the above.
   f. none of the above.
10. School conditions such as the lack of needed teaching resources or not having a teacher's desk in the classroom are those that
    a. are considered under the category of cooperative duties in workload formulas.

b. are ones that have been found not to be such that they impact on teacher load.
c. are ones that come under the Douglass formula for cooperatives or [(5 × R) × 5].
d. are ones that are not considered *in any of the load formulas* discussed in the chapter.
e. none of the above.

ANSWERS TO THE QUIZ

1. The answer to question #1, "When the 'evidence' of the teacher's workload is fully understood," is "d," that is, the evidence of teacher workload can be used to compare teacher workload toward the objective of gaining load equity among the faculty. Workload assignments have been found to differ substantially among teachers in schools and school districts. Teachers with the heaviest load indexes quite commonly are first-year teachers. It seems logical that first-year teachers be given reasonable workload assignments that give due consideration to reasonable cooperative duties along with class assignments.

    First-year teachers have been found to be a considerable percentage of those that leave the school and/or the teaching profession altogether after only the first year of service. After five years, statistical studies have revealed that 20% to 30% of teachers resign from the school district and often from the profession. Special attention must be directed to the resolution of this major problem. The current COVID-19 pandemic has added to the teacher workload problem in negative ways. Revolutionary solutions to this problem must be found; just getting back to normal will not resolve the problem. Later chapters of the book focus on this matter.

2. The answer to question #2, "The application of teacher load formulas, such as the Douglass formula," is "b," that is, "can be beneficial in explaining teacher load assignments to faculty personnel."

    If a teacher's workload is indeed on the heavy side for all teachers, the administrative action needed is to do what is possible to equate that problem. On the other hand, a teacher who is "complaining" about their workload, and if it is reasonable and close to the average of the workloads for the entire faculty, then explaining that teacher's load to them in relation to the school's overall load indices is a positive action. Quite often, it is what the teacher is doing "outside" of their required responsibilities that is causing a teacher's workload problems. Also, climate school problems, student problems or other emotional related problems are present and need to be addressed.

48   Chapter 2

3. The answer to question #3, "Teacher with the lower (20–24 indices) workloads, according to basic research studies, are likely to view the load as being"
   a. heavy 75% of the time.
   b. unreasonable 75% of the time.
   c. reasonable 75% of the time.
   d. light 75% of the time.
   e. none of the above.

   In fact, the answer is "e," that is, none of the above. In one study, reported in the chapter, 18 of 160 teachers with workloads indices of 20–24 viewed their workloads as being heavy; 5 teachers with the lowest load indices stated that their loads were "extra" heavy. In such instances, it seems quite possible that such teachers were facing special classroom problems that interfere with productive teaching results. Does the teacher have a "special" group of learners in their subject areas of teaching? What in-service help might these teachers need at this time? Are there other personal problems whereby personal counseling is needed? Are students in his or her classes in a learning atmosphere? What is the climate within the school overall? School climate is discussed in-depth in the following chapter.

4. The answer to question #4, "The SGC in the Douglass Teacher Load Formula stands for" is 'c,' that is, "subject grade coefficient." The use of the SGC gives additional credit for the several curriculum offerings. Each subject requires certain "special" preparation activities, but such preparation is not the same for all subjects. The individuals that established the SGC concept found that the major subjects required very similar special resource/activity effort. A 1.0 SGC multiplier does not change the value of the teacher's workload; an SGC of 1.3 that is given for teachers of agriculture does increase the workload of an agriculture teacher. This teacher's teaching must often take place in field. Special equipment and resources are needed for instructing different lessons. Three SGC examples: Each of the three teachers has the same basic load index. The SGC multiplier makes a "sizeable" difference in each teacher's workload.

   Art teacher with a basic teacher load of 32.31 and SGC of 1.0: TL = 32.31

   English teacher with a basic load of 32.31 and SGC of 1.1: TL = 35.54

   Agriculture teacher with a basic load of 32.31 and SGC of 1.3 = 42.00

5. The answer to question #5, "A primary reason for calculating the teachers' workload is to" is "d," that is, to determine the fairness of the faculty members' workloads and correct the workloads whereby obvious inequities exist. Although workload indices will always differ, major differences can be detected directly when all teachers' indices are assessed

Calculating and Assessing the Workload of Teacher Personnel   49

and evaluated. In some cases, certain load components such as coaching, performing, and supervision receive addition pay. When this is the case, at least two options are among the administration actions. The "teacher" is paid additionally for the extra assignment or other teaching responsibilities are reduced.

6. The answer to question #6, 'Which factor is not a component of the Douglass Teacher Load Formula?" is "f," that is, none of the above. The several load components not mentioned in the question include the SGC and the duplication factor. As noted throughout chapter 2, the components of the Douglass formula are quite comprehensive, although personal emotional and climate conditions factors are not included in the Douglass and other teacher load formulas that have been developed over the years. It seems quite possible that a load component such as an SPC (special student class) could be determined by research and serve to increase the applicability of the Douglass and other load formulas. Teaching a class of special education students or a course at the high school level for college credit could warrant credit for a teacher's workload.

7. The answer to question #7, "The Norton/Bria teacher load formula" is "c," that is, "measures the number of hours secondary teachers work each week." Unlike the Douglas Teacher Load Formula and other formulas that center on secondary school teachers, no standard grade component has been established for the various elementary school grades 1 through 6. That is, is there a load factor that differs within the elementary school grades? A quality research study of this question could serve as a great improvement for the Norton/Bria elementary teacher load formula."

8. The answer to question #8, "Although the Douglass Teacher Load Formula establishes an index number that can be utilized for equalizing teacher loads, it does not . . ." is "d," that is, "include a factor for the climate of the school which the teacher is teaching."

   Since school climate is a condition that exists within each school and all members of a school are facilitators of that climate, just how climate might be incorporated into a workload formula is not easily determined. The makeup of students in each of the teacher's classes, however, could be assessed and evaluated and utilized as a positive factor for determining a teacher's workload. This contention is addressed additionally in chapter 3.

9. The answers to question #9, "Which characteristic(s) below is/are *not measured* in either the Douglass or Norton/Bria teacher load formulas:" are "a" and "b," that is, "teacher's emotions regarding the teacher's workload" and "teacher's concept of job satisfaction."

   Various studies of teacher load have revealed how various emotional/effective characteristics affect the work of humans. School, parent, home, and family problems have been found to influence a teacher's attitude and workload conditions. Teachers are humans and experience the ups and downs as do all of us. Although chapter 2 does consider the "emotional" side of teacher load, research on this topic needs to be enlarged and updated. Along with the offering of teacher absences for illness and special emergencies, what workload considerations are in place, if any, for healing with a teacher's special needs?

Although the COVID-19 pandemic has changed the teacher's workday schedule considerably, it has not been just a matter of doing online what has been done for years in the classroom. Changes of all kinds have found their way into a teacher's workload and workday. Open then closed, then opened again and closed again have been one pattern of school operations for many schools throughout the nation. What is happening to student learning is yet to be determined. What changes are working or should we ask, "What changes have resulted in continued learning for all students?"

10. The answer to question #10, "School conditions such as the lack of needed teaching resources or not having a teacher's desk in the classroom are those that" is "d," "are ones that are not considered *in any of the load formulas* discussed in the chapter." This important answer makes one wonder about the lack of resources in today's online classes during the pandemic, although students do have pictures of various instructional resources being used by the teacher during online learning classes.

Of course, for many students, the lack of resources for learning online is one of the major problems facing them today. Through online learning, students are able to see and hear the instructor as well as see "pictures" of other students in the class. The learners are seldom in a classroom, but can connect with the class, instructor, and other class members when at home, in a library, at a picnic table, or most any other convenient place. Nevertheless, the effectiveness of online learning varies considerably. The variability of resources, along with effective supervision, are primary problem.

The availability of a vaccine for the COVID-19 virus, according to some authorities, is on its way for public vaccinations. If this becomes a reality, then the school doors will reopen and students will return to a "normal" school environment. Collaboration, cooperation, and communication will come back into play. School climate once again looms important for effective human relationships. Organizational climate is the main topic of discussion in chapter 3 that follows.

DISCUSSION QUESTIONS

1. Equity is a topic that is given considerable attention in the profession of teaching. In one sense, load equity has been given consideration at the

secondary school level by having each teacher teach five classes each day in their subject area. Although there are variations in this arrangement, in most every secondary school nationally, most teachers do teach five classes each day for five days each week. Give thought to how this arrangement might be changed toward the objective of fostering load equity for all teachers in the school and school district.
2. Measuring teacher workload at the elementary school level is accomplished by implementing the Norton/Bria workload formula. Give thought to how this strategy might serve toward resolving the equity problems that do exist. The common workweek in many businesses and industries is the 40-hour workweek. Assume that the teachers' association in your school district has recommended a compensation that calls for a 40-hour workweek with extra hourly compensation for overtime. As a school principal, you are asked to speak on this proposal at the next faculty meeting. Take a few minutes to outline your remarks for that session.
3. At the monthly faculty meeting, one of your teacher's comments that "it isn't the workload that looms important here, it is the quality of the teaching that really matters." Most professions use compensation to reward exemplary performance. One-half of the faculty at the meeting, "softly booed" the comment. As school principal, what is your action or response at this time?

KEY CHAPTER IDEAS AND RECOMMENDATIONS

- The topic of teacher workload extends far beyond the concept of class size. Although the number of students in the classes taught is of importance, other load components are of major importance as well.
- Teacher workload inequities result in a number of problems. The problems of "teacher loss" from the school and from teaching are problems that effect student learning. Teacher retention in the profession continues to be a national concern.
- The ability to "measure" teacher workload has been available for several decades. Formulas for assessing teaching load have been developed by several authorities. However, administrative preparation programs have failed to give teacher workload the attention it needs and therefore it is seldom put into practice in local schools. At the secondary school level, the assignment of five classes per day is a common practice for teachers. However, load components include many other factors that must be considered in attempts to gain load equality.
- School conditions such as having access to needed instructional resources, having a teacher's desk in the classroom, and having "reasonable"

cooperative duties are of primary importance in the consideration of improving workload equity among the teaching faculty.
- School working conditions, commonly viewed as school climate, have major effects on teacher workload.
- Unfortunately, studies of teacher workload have regularly revealed that a school's best teachers have the greatest workload index ratings. When the best teachers consistently are given the highest workloads, their teaching ability can turn to an actual level of mediocrity.
- It is not uncommon for teachers with the lightest load indices to feel that they are carrying heavy workloads. Having statistical load data for teacher workloads on hand serves the positive purpose of being able to counsel the teacher relative to the actual status of his or her "true" workload.
- Although several teacher workload formulas have been developed over the years, the Douglass teacher workload formula has been implemented most often in local schools. Efforts to equalize teacher workloads can foster improved teaching and, in turn, improved student learning. In addition, workload equity can serve to lessen teacher burnout and teacher loss from the profession.

REFERENCES

Douglass, H. R. (1951). The 1950 revision of the Douglass high school teacher load formula. *NASSP Bulletin*, 35, 13–14.

Norton, M.S. (1959). Teacher load in Nebraska high schools in cities from 5,000 to 25,000 population. Unpublished doctoral dissertation, Department of Educational Administration and Supervision, University of Nebraska, Lincoln.

Norton, M.S., and Bria, R. (1992). Toward an equitable measure of elementary school teacher load. *Record in Educational Administration and Supervision*, 13(1), 62–66.

Chapter 3

School Climate and Its Influence on Teacher Workload

Primary chapter goal: To underscore the importance of school climate and its influence on the school teacher's workload.

What does school climate have to do with teacher workload and ultimately the teacher's classroom performance?

The "short" answer is *everything*. Organizational climate is defined commonly as the collective personality of the school: the atmosphere as characterized by the social and professional interactions of the individuals in the school. We often speak of an individual's personality. The "personality" of a school has been termed the school's "syntality." School climate is interpersonal; it is reflected in the relationships, attitudes, and actions of the professional staff in the school setting (Norton & Kelly, 1997).

School climate is significant in a discussion of teacher workload for several reasons. The volumes of literature that exist on the topic of burnout tend to focus on the conditions that constitute the workplace as opposed to the amount of work that is required. The amount of work required is conditioned by the climate that surrounds it. That is, emotional exhaustion comes about by the demands of the job and the individual's confidence in being able to achieve the work.

SCHOOL CLIMATE DEFINED

School climate is defined as the collective personality of the school: the atmosphere as characterized by the social and professional interactions of the individuals in the school. We often speak of an individual's personality. School climate is interpersonal; it is reflected in the relationships, attitudes, and actions of the professional staff in the school setting.

School climate is significant in a discussion of teacher workload for several reasons:

1) The climate of the school sets the tone for the human considerations important for meeting school goals and objectives and resolving related problems.
2) Effective school communication necessitates a climate of trust, mutual respect, and clarity of function. Communication serves to tie the school personnel together; without communication, human energies are not properly focused.
3) A positive climate sets the opportunity for personnel growth. Personnel growth is essential for schools to remain alive and vital.
4) School climate conditions the setting for creative personal growth which is essential for the presence of human satisfaction, feelings of confidence of one's worth, and successful achievement of one's work.
5) Along with a climate that serves to stimulate cooperative staff efforts, positive school climates add to the human objective of helping faculty personnel to live better lives by ameliorating emotional problems and promoting guidance that fosters growth and development (Norton & Kelly, 1997).

A LIGHTBULB EXPERIENCE

Paul had served as a fighter pilot for the U.S. Air Force and upon his discharge from the service, he became the chief engineer for a large telephone and telegraph company in a Midwestern state. Each year, the local school district had a program named "Scientist for Teacher Day." For one day each year, local "scientists" from various leading companies in the city came to the schools and served as a teacher for the day.

The regular school teachers took the opportunity to take part in various program development meetings in their special field of teaching. The visiting scientist taught in each of five classes over the day. They did not teach the lessons that the teacher would have presented, rather they spoke about their special businesses and their importance in community development and operations. In most cases, the scientist emphasized the importance of education for success in their fields. In most cases, the importance of knowing science, mathematics, social science, and civic relations was emphasized.

At the close of the school day and the "teaching" of five classes, the school curriculum coordinator met Paul at the classroom door and they walked slowly to the teachers' lounge for refreshments. As Paul and the coordinator entered the lounge, Paul plunged down into the softest chair in the room, and said, "Good heavens, do teachers do this every day?" Of course, Paul did not know that the five-class day every week was indeed ongoing or that the extra cooperative duties of a teacher are added to this workload.

WHAT BASIC RESEARCH STUDIES HAVE REVEALED REGARDING SCHOOL CLIMATE AND JOB PERFORMANCE

Several studies over the years have found that secondary school teachers were unable to carry out their tasks when the climate in the school was unhealthy. A negative school climate tends to add to the workload of school faculty personnel and inhibits productive energies that are needed for meeting stated purposes.

Studies have found that the general causes of teacher stress and burnout are related to a lack of strong leadership and a negative school climate, as well as ongoing increases in workload requirements. Personnel contend with negative working conditions for a time and then often deal with the climate conditions by "soldiering," increasing their absenteeism, or resigning from the organization. Soldiering is the practice of going through the motions but not actually doing the work. The military command of "in-step march" has the soldier marching in step but remaining in place.

A leader of one education organization commented that "workload was one of the biggest threats to teacher recruitment and retention" (Stewart, 2020). Although the given tasks were viewed as important, the volume of the tasks was felt to be unmanageable. Required exam forms, administrative tasks, behavioral monitoring, data tracking, student work marking, and extended meeting requirements were responsibilities named as contributing to long hours of work and unmanageable workloads. Teacher workload is not just related to the teacher's work in the classroom, but encompasses all of the work responsibilities that the teacher must perform.

As noted by Stanley (2014), unsustainable workloads are destroying the quality of teaching. He noted that 91% of school teachers have expressed stress in recent years while 74% suffered anxiety due to excessive workloads. Eighty percent of the teachers reported that their mental health could be improved if workload could be reduced. How bad is the situation? As one teacher reported, "After ten years of outstanding teaching, I have decided to leave the profession, the workload is unbearable and is ripping my family apart."

SCHOOL CLIMATES DO DIFFER

When attempting to improve the workload of the school teachers, the action tends to focus on the reduction of class size. What needs to be assessed and evaluated is the school's climate. However, climates in schools do differ and that difference is what looms important. As one professor stated in his administration class, "There are two kinds of leadership, Good and Bad!"

Various climate conditions are discussed in chapter 3, beginning with the two basic climate types of good "open climates" and bad "closed climates." An open climate is viewed as having 'functional flexibility" while a "closed climate" is distinguished by "functional rigidity." In an open climate, leadership is demonstrated by various sources of the organization. Cooperative decision-making and high morale among the workers are in evidence. Job satisfaction is at a high level that facilitates the attainment of stated purposes. Workers gain personal satisfaction by helping to achieve the overall school goals.

THE IMPORTANCE OF A HEALTHY LEARNING CLIMATE FOR STUDENTS DURING THE PANDEMIC

Schools, departments, and online teachers, like normal school settings, are staffed by people and effective learning climates in any situation are a human condition. The kind of climate that exists in a virtual learning environment requires attention to the human resources that are involved in the process. School leaders must give primary attention to the inhibitors and facilitators of learning effectiveness in each situation (e.g., classrooms, online, and other virtual learning situations). What are the determinants that are effective student learning set the stage for dealing with the determinants of strategies for planning and delivering learning in the environment on hand? How best can the determinants be implemented in each situation?

The learning abilities of students differ and so do the situations in which virtual learning takes place. In some instances, parents are in a positive position to help serve as "mentors" for their child's program. In other cases, a qualified mentor is required. Although the following case involves a university student in his first semester of an engineering program, his learning record reveals what can be done with high quality teacher/mentors. The student's program of studies included "difficult" courses in mathematics and science. Mentoring was practiced on a daily basis. After semester one, the student was named on the dean's list with grades of four A's and one B+. A special case for sure. Nevertheless, virtual learning along with high quality teacher/mentor services has high potential for successful learning results.

THE IMPORTANCE OF ADMINISTRATIVE LEADERSHIP

Although the school principal is a diligent worker, he or she does not have to keep pushing for more effort on the part of the faculty and staff. Cooperative decision-making is evident among the school members and collaborative work achievements are present. The school principal sets an example by working cooperatively with individuals and groups within the school. The teaching staff enjoys a high level of job satisfaction; bickering and griping among the workers are not in evidence. Both the teaching faculty and the school leadership tend to use the term "we" when speaking about the school's accomplishments.

Things tend to be quite different in closed school climates. Group members obtain little satisfaction in either task-achievement or social needs. School leaders are ineffective in directing the activities of the teachers and are not inclined to be aware of workload conditions or other problems related to personal welfare. Emphasis is placed on work production. The statement, "Let's each give just 10% more" is a common request. On the other hand, open climates have been associated with the positive implementation of innovations in school settings in the large majority of research studies that have taken place in schools historically.

To understand more fully the effects of school climate on work and work conditions, it is necessary to know more about the facts of school climate and its variations in which workers are engaged. As previously noted, one might say that there are two kinds of school climate, good and bad, but this view falls short of the mark. The four primary types of climate are set forth in the following section. Keep in mind that the interest here resides in thinking/knowing how each type of climate conditions the atmosphere in which the school faculty and students are "working."

CLIMATE TYPES AND THEIR EFFECTS ON SCHOOL HUMAN RESOURCES

The terms commonly used to identify the terminal points of the school climate continuum are "open" and "closed." The open climate is described by what has been termed as "functional flexibility" and closed climates are distinguished by "functional rigidity." The large majority of research studies on school climates have found that open climates tend to open the door for more and improved innovations that center on the improvement of student learning.

In an open climate, leadership acts can emerge easily from all sources within the organization. The faculty enjoys extremely high morale and everyone works well together without complaining and pointing fingers. Faculty members hold high levels of job satisfaction and possess the incentives to work things out and move positively toward the accomplishment of positive school goals and purposes. The school principal sets an example by working diligently himself or herself and does not have to "preach" about keeping up high production. The welfare of the school's human resources is of high priority.

In a closed climate, the school faculty members obtain little satisfaction in regard to either task-achievement or important social needs. Ineffective leadership on the part of the school principal is revealed in the neglect of looking out for the faculty's personal welfare. Group collaboration is minimal; the major outlet for the teachers is vested in the completion of a variety of required reports and marking requirements that seem to be always increasing. A favorite request that commonly is voiced by school leaders is for the faculty "to give just 10% more effort toward the work production requirements of the school." However, such a request tends to be voiced quite often.

It has been noted previously that the factors that constitute teacher load go far beyond the single consideration of class size. A more comprehensive perspective is set forth as follows: it divides load factors into nine major areas relating to the types of duties that teachers actually perform.

LOAD FACTORS

Pupils and classes
    Class size
    Number of special needs pupils
    Number of different subjects
    Total number of pupils
    Type of pupils
Plant facilities
    Overcrowded classrooms
    Lack of equipments
    Lack of supplies
    Lack of books
    Poor school conditions
Plans and preparations
    Daily lesson plans
    Preparation of materials
    Planning excursions, and so on
    Collaborative planning sessions
Changing emphasis in education program
    Implementation of changing philosophies
    Marking and completing increasing reports
    Ongoing testing and grading
    Frequency of school principal turnover

Administration and clerical work
    Committee assignments
    Ongoing teacher development programs
    "Red tape" accounting requirements
    Increasing clerical work
    Class interruptions for a variety of activities
    Out-of-class pupil supervision
    Care of classroom equipment/ conditions
Extracurricular duties
    After-school student activities/ sponsorships
    Community, student group activities
    Lunchroom/playground supervision
    Parent/teacher group sessions/ activities
Guidance and adjustment
    Individual student counseling
    Keeping student records
    Mentoring services, guidance for new teachers

Parental conferences
Student discipline conferences/ supervision
Public relations activities
  PTA meetings, conferences
  Civic and social services
  Drives, campaigns, negotiations
Contests, games, plays, and so on
Professional improvement
Continuous education improvement
Curriculum development groups
Summer school-related education activities

The foregoing listing of job load factors does mention class size as one of the many factors that add to a teacher's workload. However, we emphasize the point that teacher load and class size are not synonymous; class size is only one factor that adds to the overall work of the teacher. In fact, class size has been found to have direct effect on pupil learning. Various studies have concluded that class size does contribute to a teacher's workload, but it is only one factor, among many, that make up the load of the teacher. It seems only reasonable that smaller class sizes would be less "stressful" than larger class sizes.

Although people differ, the factors that affect teacher load tend to differ as well. For example, factors that serve to promote workload strain and pressure can be traced to specific teaching requirements; other factors that are required outside the classroom might serve as the primary sources for teacher workload pressures. The results of one study found several general factors that constituted the workload for both male and female teachers. Two such factors were strain and pressure. *Strain* commonly is defined as a force tending to pull or stretch something to an extreme or damaging degree. *Pressure*, in relation to workload, is viewed as the burden of physical or mental distress that is experienced by an individual.

In one study, nine factors that caused some degree of strain and/or pressure were as follows:

a. Load due to the number or type of students: 38% of men teachers and 22% of women teachers reported considerable pressure/strain.
b. Load due to the inadequacy of school facilities: 38% of men teachers and 41% of women teachers reported considerable pressure/strain.
c. Load due to requirements of instructional planning only and class preparation: 37% of men teachers and 41% of women teachers reported considerable pressure/strain.
d. Load due to changing emphasis in classroom methods and procedures: 38% of men teachers and 42% of women teachers reported considerable pressure/strain.
e. Load due to clerical and administrative work: 38% of men teachers and 30% of women teachers reported considerable pressure/strain.

60   Chapter 3

   f. Load due to requirements of extracurricular responsibilities: 38% of men teachers and 41% of women teachers reported considerable pressure/strain.
      Load due to due to guidance and pupil-adjustment responsibilities: 38% of men teachers and 41% of women teachers reported considerable pressure/strain.
   h. Load due to guidance and pupil-adjustment responsibilities: 38% of men teachers and 41% of women teachers reported considerable pressure/strain.
   i. Load due to required community relations: 38% of men teachers and 41% of women teachers reported considerable pressure/strain.
   j. Load due to professional improvement requirements: 38% of men teachers and 42% of women teachers reported considerable pressure/strain.

The foregoing summary of factors that affect teachers' workload serves to underscore the extensive nature of teacher activities and responsibilities that constitute the "make up" of a teacher's workload. Make special note of the fact that only one entry, "a," deals specifically with class size. This important fact has been underscored previously in chapters 1 and 2; class size, although of considerable importance, is only one of many factors/conditions that influence the workload of the professional teaching staff. In addition, many of the factors that influence the teacher's workload are not included in the various workload formulas that have been developed over the years.

HOW IS ORGANIZATIONAL/SCHOOL CLIMATE MEASURED?

Much of the important research on school climate took place six decades ago. For example, in 1962, Halpin and Croft developed a climate "instrument" that became the leading instrument for measuring school climate. One could not count the number of research studies that have utilized the Organizational Climate Description Questionnaire (OCDQ) for measuring climate in school settings. Doctoral dissertations by the dozens centered on climate studies during the 1960s and 1970s.

Christian's doctoral dissertation completed in 1972, *Organizational Climate of Elementary Schools and the Introduction and Utilization of Innovative Educational Practices*, is one such example. This study focused on the relationship between organizational climate and the rate of introduction and utilization of innovation educational practices in the public elementary schools. A statistically significant positive relationship was found between openness of organizational climate and the rate of introduction in and utilization of innovative educational practices in the schools.

The OCDQ consists of a number of Likert-type items that focus on how teachers perceive the climate in their schools. Eight subtests are included that relate to school principal and teacher behaviors. Two of these behaviors are disengagement and intimacy. *Disengagement* refers to the teachers' tendency of not being meaningfully involved in the activities that are taking place. That is, they might be going through the motions of the tasks being confronted, but are not acting meaningfully in fulfilling them. *Intimacy* centers on the extent to which faculty personnel and others in the school enjoy their relationships with one another.

In discussing school climate, the conditions of open and closed climates are most often considered. Open climates are described commonly by the terms of environment, synergy, equilibrium, and equifinality. For example, in schools where an open climate exists, the morale is high and the faculty and staff work well together. Cooperative decision-making is practiced. On the other hand, in a closed school system, communication is "bound up" with negativism and socialization among the faculty is limited at best. Workers commonly are "going through the motions" of working together, but the tasks at hand are not being accomplished.

YES, THE QUALITY OF A SCHOOL'S CLIMATE CAN BE MEASURED

At this time, here and now, it is somewhat difficult to explain how school climate is measured. School programming is being carried out during the pandemic by virtual means even though criticism is being directed toward the process. Many schools have closed, reopened, and then closed again. Homeschooling reportedly has been poorly supervised and as one school leader commented, "Students are not learning." Parental supervision of their child's learning reportedly is failing. Many parents are working from home and have their own work responsibilities to perform. In one report, a father held a major in mathematics education. Nevertheless, his final college math course was calculus 101. His son took that course in high school. Dad was not prepared to give his son much help in calculus 102.

Over the years several "quality" measuring instruments have been developed. As previously noted, the OCDQ, developed by Halpin and Croft in 1962, is one instrument that has been widely used by schools nationally for assessing school climate. Other worthy climate assessment instruments include the following: the High School Climate Index (HSCI) developed by Stern (1964); the Purdue Teacher Opinionnaire (PTO) developed by Bentley and Rempel in 1980; the CFK Ltd. School Climate Profile published by Charles F. Kettering in 1973; the Harrison Instrument for Diagnosing Organizational Ideology developed by Harrison in 1985; and the Organizational Health Inventory (OHI-S) developed by Hoy, Tarter and Kottkamp in 1991, which was revised later by Hoy and Clover.

Other versions of the OCDQ were developed for the elementary and middle schools. Such measuring tools have been termed surveys, scales, context inventories, and trust scales. A partial example of a climate assessment instrument that might be developed for a school is illustrated as follows. This "incomplete example" might be extended to include additional major sections such as Student Staff Relationships, Student Behavior Rules, Peer Relationships, and Student Achievement/Learning Environment. The need is for the school staff to complete a climate assessment tool that fits the situation at hand.

SCHOOL IMPROVEMENT CLIMATE INVENTORY

The School_____

The Grades_____

Directions: Circle the number on the right that best describes how you view your school or one for which you are most familiar. Do not circle more than one number for each statement.

Value of each number from 1 to 5:

(1) Strongly disagree, (2) Disagree, (3) Don't know, (4) Agree, (5) Strongly agree

A. School Atmosphere
  1. Our school has a healthful/friendly climate   1 2 3 4 5
  2. Our school is a place where student can learn in a
     pleasant atmosphere   1 2 3 4 5
  3. The faculty and students take pride in the quality of
     our school   1 2 3 4 5
  4. Students in our school speak highly of the
     environment in which they learn   1 2 3 4 5
  5. Students and faculty in our school work cooperatively
     to get things accomplished   1 2 3 4 5

B. Student/Teacher Relationships
  1. Staff members and students trust and respect one
     another   1 2 3 4 5
  2. Teachers in our school care about students and go
     out of their way to help them   1 2 3 4 5
  3. Teachers and other personnel in our school treat
     students fairly and as individuals   1 2 3 4 5

Specific entries in the assessment survey that revealed positive climate feelings should be extended. Those entries that revealed climate areas needing improvement should be reassessed and evaluated. The measurement tools are available, the need is to use them. An improved climate depends on what positive actions are assessed, evaluated, discussed, and improved. Improvements will focus on needed change. Schools are people and changes in people are the "without which not" of climate improvement. As noted by Follett, "The central problem of any enterprise is the building and maintaining of dynamic yet harmonious human relationships" (1924).

A LOOK AT HOW COVID-19 HAS CHANGED THE CLIMATE FOR TEACHING

Just what actions should be taken for promoting student learning during the COVID-19 pandemic are not yet clear. During the past several months, and as previously noted, schools have closed and remained closed, closed and then reopened, reopened and then closed once again. Virtual teaching has been in place in many school districts and many teachers have made the decision to retire or to just leave the teaching profession for good. Those teachers who have continued to "teach" during COVID-19 have voiced their opinions relative to the pandemic's effects on their teaching.

In reviewing a wide range of literature on the topic, both positive and negative changes in teaching have been expressed by those remaining in the profession. Although the teaching experiences have taken place in different ways and many different schools, we note below that some positive outcomes for teachers have been identified. In the following section, several positive outcomes and several negative outcomes of teachers who are or have been teaching during the pandemic are set forth below. We start by listing positive outcomes/changes related to teaching performance.

Changes in Teaching during COVID-19—Teachers' Responses

a. The vital importance of teacher/student relationships has been one of the most rewarding revelations for me. The "old" adage of knowing your students has taken on new meanings for me. One-on-one sessions with a student, without question, result in learning about the student's real interests and needs. A big change for me has been my efforts to relate my teaching, in the best way that I can, to the student's success level.
b. Teaching during the pandemic has brought about one factor that we have talked about for many years, that of cooperation and collaboration. The

pandemic has brought about the absolute need to collaborate with my colleagues and gain a meaningful communication relationship with other teachers and the parents of my students. For me, it isn't just something that we do, rather it is something that we all know is needed if our students are to be successful in learning culture. I really cannot explain it as clearly as I might, but cooperation is just something as a thing that we should do, rather it is a relationship that must be ongoing with the goal of better teaching and improved student learning.

c. During my four years of preparing for the work of a classroom teacher, I remember hearing the phrase "know your students" over and over again. Knowing your students meant that it was important to know the learning needs of students and possibly how they learn the best. I guess that I viewed the phrase as meaning that it was important to be friendly and caring as a teacher. Certainly, there isn't anything wrong with that point of view, but teaching during COVID-19 has brought about a deeper meaning of the phrase.

One of my university professors emphasized the fact that students are different. He underscored the fact that students have different talents, interests, and physical abilities. What I have found to be missing in this important contention is the fact that students have greatly differing home/family experiences.

Most students have fathers and mothers, but many do not have both and some have neither. I have kept asking myself, what education/learning does each of my students have from long associations with persons at his home or some other home. These differences certainly have an impact on a student's motivation and attitude toward learning. I keep asking myself the question, "What kinds of learning might I give each student that serves in some way to meet the 'missing learning' that others have benefited at home?"

d. I have 16 years of classroom teaching and must admit that teaching virtually has been difficult for me. The newer teachers seem to be doing OK but they were "brought up" with all the new technology that I am trying to learn in just a few weeks. No, I am not enjoying virtual teaching and it appears that it will even be extended when the pandemic is over. In short, I really do not enjoy my teaching days at this time and have thought about stepping out several times in the last three months. The comment "know your pupils" is more than difficult with virtual teaching. In the regular classroom situation, I could really get to know my students. Today, I might pass them on the street even after the need for a mask is over.

e. Teaching just isn't any fun for me anymore.

f. In my situation, I feel that I am more in charge of my teaching than was possible in the regular classroom with so many "everyday" policy changes. I feel that I have far more control of what and how I present my lessons. As yet, I have received some mandate every day to change or do something that someone else wants done. Since the principal and other administrators apparently do not know what is best to do, I have been able to do what I have found most effective and beneficial for students in my virtual classes.

IMPROVING THE SCHOOL CLIMATE UNDER NEW PROGRAM CONDITIONS

The improvement of school climate, at this time in history, might be named more appropriately with the title of education climate. The closing and reopening of schools during the pandemic brought about new environments for the teaching of students. Even though some schools remained open, the practices needed for dealing with the COVID-19 virus necessitate changes in the physical environments of the school students. In most situations, schools must comply with the distance, sanitation, and face mask requirements that commonly are being required of schools in most states of the union.

Leadership actions needed for climate improvement necessitate the assessment of the areas needing improvement, planning and implementing, guiding improvement objectives, establishing work responsibilities for administering the plan, and controlling the improvement process "along the way" rather than attempting to do so at the end of the school year. What leadership actions have been taken for implementing the strategies and controlling the improvement process? To what extent has the entire teaching faculty been actively involved in the improvement plan? Have improvement activities actually resulted in climate improvements? If the answers to such questions are "yes," why were these activities so positive and how might they be additionally extended?

One thing appears to be certain. Climate improvement projects cannot be successful without the actual support of parents. This fact does not mean that parents should only be aware of the climate improvement plan of the school and have opportunities to ask questions about it. Rather, parents should be directly involved in the early planning phases of the improvement plan and be meaningfully involved in the implementation of the plan by understanding their responsibilities for fostering the objectives of the plan in the home. In short, schools are not successful without a strong system of support from parents (Wilmore, 1992).

During the time that school personnel were serving under what is commonly termed as "being normal times," several specific responsibilities for school leaders were highly recommended for improving school climate.

Developing a set of shared goals, fostering a positive self-image and an attitude of having high expectations for students and personnel, establishing many opportunities for fostering professional growth, developing a viable set of personnel policies and regulations, and developing a positive problem-solving capacity were the highly recommended goals for fostering a healthy school climate. The current virus pandemic has affected the accomplishment of these principles since opportunities for collaboration and face-to-face communication have been inhibited in many school situations.

The terms "school climate" and "school culture" are often misunderstood and misused. The two terms do have certain similarities or links of relationship. The improvement of school climate is conditioned by an understanding of its components and it links with the school's culture. Improvement of the climate necessitates having an understanding of what determinants make up the climate. Fox and others (1973) set forth three primary determinants of organizational climate: Program determinants, process determinants and material determinants. *Program determinants* are related to such factors as how the school provides opportunities for students to be involved in the following: active learning, the development of individualized goals and objectives for student performance, a variety of learning environments, a variety of curricular and extracurricular activities, learning experiences adjusted to the student's success level, participative decision-making activities, and in a varied system of learning rewards.

Process determinants include the evidence of having a cooperative understanding of the school's primary goals and objectives, an ability to face ongoing problems and the ability to resolve them, an effective two-way communication system, a cooperative decision-making, a human autonomy accompanied by accountability, a planned program teaching-learning strategies, and a focus on meeting today's requirements with attention to the needs of the future.

Material determinants feature the attention given to having the instructional resources needed for effective program instruction, the suitability of the school plant for instructional purposes, and the ready availability for audio-visual materials needed by teachers for effective teaching in the classroom and other instructional areas of the school.

SUCCESSFUL PROGRAM PRACTICES IN THE AREA OF SCHOOL CLIMATE CHANGES

The significance of the foregoing information is vested in the fact that school climate and the related characteristics of teacher workload are not singular considerations of class size. Improvement of school climate is affected by other successful programs and practices. One such factor is that of the need for the school to develop and implement a relevant set of shared goals that serve as the *purposes* of the school's programming. Such a purpose statement is not something that is printed on a plaque and hung on the wall of a school's hallway. It is something that the school does programmatically; it gives the program a meaningful direction (Norton, 2008).

As early as 1938, Barnard underscored the vital importance of cooperative goal setting. He stressed the fact that cooperation was essential for individuals in an organization for accomplishing its stated purposes. Mandated curriculum programs have been instituted by governmental agencies during the past several decades. Mandated programs leave little or no room for innovative student learning. Such commanding program requirements tend to inhibit cooperative program designs: ones in which the school district and individual schools have found most effective for students for meeting students' personal learning interests and needs.

HIGH QUALITY SCHOOL PROGRAMS HOLD HIGH EXPECTATIONS FOR STUDENTS

Effective school programs focus on each student's personal learning interests and needs. Although effective schools hold high expectations for each student, learning is centered on the student's success level. That is, levels of expectation are determined so that they solicit the best performance that the student has to offer. Learning goals provide the needed focus for motivating continued improvement. "Failure" tends to militate against positive improvement. On the other hand, "success" leads to student motivation and continued improvement. In addition, student success serves to foster a healthy school climate. A healthy school climate leads to a positive self-image for the school: one that reflects the purposes that the school's stakeholders expect and the school must provide.

Schools with healthy school climates provide a variety of opportunities for their human resources to grow and develop. As noted by Norton (2008), "The determination of school climate is the forerunner of the determination of the strategies for school improvement generally and improvement of conditions in the workplace specifically" (p. 236). We note the emphasis given to the school environment for determining the conditions of the school climate.

In order for the school personnel to be vital and alive, the school environment must provide a variety of ways in which the personal resources can be highly motivated toward initiatives that foster creativeness. The characteristic of creativeness looms important in that it serves toward the accomplishment of the primary purposes that have been cooperatively established.

The goals that have been established are purposeful to the extent that they provide a focus for meeting the changes that the school must face. Such a climate requires an atmosphere of trust, mutual respect, and clarity in what it is that the school personnel plan to achieve. Without the existence of these characteristics, healthy organizations have little chance of succeeding. The communication that serves to tie the organization together is supported by faculty relationships that are truly cooperative and communication strategies that are based on positive team building. That is, effective communication is characterized by mutual trust and mutual respect that exist among the faculty personnel.

In the next chapter, the topics of dealing with teacher workload during the pandemic and its effects on the human characteristics during the crisis are presented. However, the primary focus of chapter 4 centers on ways to improve teacher workload during "normal" times when students are learning in their school's classrooms. Attempts to improve the school climate when students and teachers are presently facing a variety of "restraining circumstances" are difficult at best. Nevertheless, many of the strategies that have proven beneficial for improving the school climate in "normal" times have implications for virtual learning as well.

CHAPTER 3 QUIZ

Directions: Circle the answer to each question posed. Check the correct responses at the end of the quiz.

1. The term "syntality" refers to
   a. a closed climate system.
   b. an open climate system.
   c. the personality of the school.
   d. workload factors that determine best performance.
   e. none of the above.
2. School climate, although of major importance in the determination of a teacher's workload,
   a. has yet to be scientifically measured.
   b. is a characteristic of relationships between parents and teachers.
   c. is defined as the collective personality of the school.
   d. is the degree of academic achievement revealed in the Norton climate formula.
   e. none of the above.
3. Studies have found that the general causes of teacher stress and burnout are
   a. fostered by a lack of adequate teacher preparation.

b. caused by stress and burnout related to weak leadership and a negative school climate.
   c. founded on the lack of adequate school funding.
   d. primarily due to factors outside the school environment.
   e. none of the above.
4. Teacher workload has been found to be
   a. an imaginative characteristic that accompanies feelings of inferiority.
   b. caused by poor prior preparation of the individual teacher.
   c. related to certain personality types.
   d. one of the biggest threats to teacher recruitment and retention.
   e. none of the above.
5. An open school climate is
   a. best described as being "functionally flexible."
   b. impossible to attain due to differences that always exist inside a school setting.
   c. always related to the schools with undemocratic policies and regulations.
   d. based mainly on the way school leaders give positive feedback for positive performance.
   e. none of the above.
6. It has been found by many science studies that class size
   a. is not one of the determinants causing teacher workload anxieties.
   b. is indeed the leading factor for causing teacher workload problems.
   c. should not be considered in teacher workload assessments since it is the temperament of the students, not the number of students, that adds to workload anxiety.
   d. is one factor among many that makes up the workload of the teacher.
   e. none of the above.
7. The OCDQ is
   a. the Office of Climate Determinants.
   b. the Organization of Climate Quality.
   c. the Organizational Climate Description Questionnaire.
   d. the Office of Correction for Developing Quality.
   e. none of the above.
8. The terms "school climate" and "school culture" are
   a. synonymous.
   b. similar in many ways.
   c. much different from one another definitionally.
   d. characteristics that cannot be assessed.
   e. none of the above.
9. Three primary determinants of school climate are
   a. program, process, and material determinants.

b. finance, leadership, rewards, and policy.
   c. rules, regulations, directives, and planning determinants.
   d. teacher autonomy, parental involvement, performance pay, and high praise.
   e. none of the above.
10. School goals are purposeful to the extent that
   a. they provide a focus for meeting the changes that the school must face.
   b. they are teacher products.
   c. they are approved by the school board before being implemented.
   d. they leave much room for discretional implementation.
   e. none of the above.

ANSWERS TO THE QUIZ

1. The answer to question #1, "The term 'syntality' refers to" is "c," that is, "the personality of the school."
2. The answer to question #2, "School climate, although of major importance in the determination of a teacher's workload," is "c," that is, "is defined as the collective personality of the school."
3. The answer to question #3, ".Studies have found that the general causes of teacher stress and burnout are," is "b," that is, "caused by stress and burnout related to weak leadership and negative school climate."
4. The answer to question #4, "Teacher workload has been found to be," is "d," that is, one of the biggest threats to teacher recruitment and retention." Note the paramount importance of this finding. Teacher recruitment and retention has been listed near the top of problems facing education during normal times and continues to be so during the pandemic.
5. The answer to question #5, "An open school climate is," is "a," that is, "best described as being 'functionally flexible.'"
6. The answer to question #6, "It has been found by many science studies that class size," is "d," that is, "is one factor among many that makes up the workload of the teacher."
7. The answer to question #7, "The OCDQ is," is "c," that is, "the Organizational Climate Description Questionnaire." The OCDQ is perhaps the most commonly used instrument to assess school climate in schools nationally.
8. The answer to question #8, "The terms 'school climate' and 'school culture' are," is "b," that is, "similar in many ways." Culture is the set of important beliefs and values that members of the school system share. Climate is the collective personality of a school or school system. It is the

atmosphere that prevails as characterized by the social and professional interactions of people (Norton, 2008).

9. The answer to question #9, "Three primary determinants of school climate are" is "a," that is, "program, process, and material determinants."
10. The answer to question #10, "School goals are purposeful to the extent that" is "a," that is, "they provide a focus for making the changes that the school must face." Effective and successful schools give serious thought and attention to the goals and objectives that their learning programs will address.

QUIZ SCORING RESULTS

10–9 correct answers: ***** five bright shining stars
8–7 correct answers: **** four shining stars
6–5 correct answers: *** three stars
4–3 correct answers: ** two fading stars
2–1 correct answers: * one dim star
0 correct answers: *one falling star

KEY CHAPTER IDEAS AND RECOMMENDATIONS

- Although class size is among the conditions that make up teacher workload, many other factors/conditions weigh heavily on the total workload of the school teacher.
- School climate is defined as the collective personality of the school; the atmosphere as defined by the social and professional interactions of the individuals in the school.
- The climate of the school sets the tone for human consideration important for meeting school goals and resolving related problems.
- A negative climate adds to the workload of the faculty personnel and inhibits productive energies needed to meet stated purposes.
- Workload has been viewed as being one of the biggest threats to teacher recruitment and retention.
- Open climates facilitate healthy work environments and workloads are viewed as being reduced and less distracting in such environments.
- Workload factors come from many sources: pupils and classes, plant facilities, plans and preparation, changing purposes, administrative leadership, and extracurricular responsibilities.
- Research findings have revealed that, when the climate is unhealthy, teachers are unable to carry out their tasks.

- Strong leadership is needed for healthy open climates to exist.
- Strain and pressure are two factors that influence workloads for teachers. These two characteristics are recognizable, perhaps, but workload measuring formulas have yet to find a way to include these conditions.
- Goals and purposes of education remain important in educational programming during the virus pandemic.
- School climate is determined by three primary conditions: program, process, and material. Climate improvement must focus on these factors.
- The goals that are established for the school are purposeful to the extent that they provide a focus for meeting the changes that the school must face.

REFERENCES

Barnard, C. I., (1938). *The functions of the executive.* Cambridge, MA: Harvard University Press.

Christian, C. F. (1972). *Organizational climate of elementary schools and the introduction and utilization of innovative practices.* Unpublished doctoral dissertation. University of Nebraska, Lincoln.

Follett, M. P. (1924). *Creative Experience.* New York: Longmans, Green.

Fox, R. S., et. al. (1973). School climate improvement: A challenge to the school administrator. Phi Delta Kappa.

Halpin, A., & Croft, D. B. (1962). *The Organization Climate of Schools.* U.S. Office of Education Research Project (Contract # SAE 543-8639). Chicago: University of Chicago, Midwest Administration Center.

Harrison, R. (1985). *The Handbook for Group Facilitation.* Newton, MA: Development Research Associates.

Hoy, W. K., & Clover, S. I. R. (1986). Elementary school climate: A revision of the OCDQ. *Elementary Administration Quarterly,* 22, 93–110.

Norton, M. S. (2008). *Human Resources Administration for Educational Leaders.* SAGE, Los Angeles, CA.

Norton, M. S., & Kelly, L. K. (1997). *Resource Allocation: Managing Money and People.* Eye on Education, Inc., Larchmont, N.Y.

Stanley, J. (2014). How unsustainable workloads are destroying the quality of teaching. From the web: https: //schoolweek.co.uk/how-unsustainable-workloads/

Stern, G. G. (1964). *High School Characteristics Index.* Syracuse, NKY: Psychological Research Center, Syracuse, New York.

Stewart, W. (2018). *Teacher Workload 'Unmanageable', Dfe Study Finds.* Tes News. On the web: https://www.tes.com/news/teacher-workload-unmanageable-dfe-study-finds

Wilmore, H. J. (1992). The "affective" middle school: Keys to a nurturing school climate. *Schools in the Middle.* 1 (4), 31–34.

Chapter 4

The Primary Recommendations for Improving Teacher Workload

Primary chapter goal: To set forth recommended practices for improving the teacher load problems facing schools nationally.

The topic of improving the workload of teachers has always been a difficult problem to resolve, but the problem of facing a virus pandemic has changed the instructional procedures for most teachers in America's schools. Open schools, closed schools, homeschooling, and other virtual strategies have altered the components that make up the workload of teacher personnel. In a normal school setting, it is typical for the secondary school teacher to prepare for and to teach five classes of one/two subjects each day. Each class has a range of students commonly from 15 to 25 in number.

The elementary school teacher, in normal settings, commonly has 25 pupils and teaches grade/level material 6 hours each day. Of course, both elementary and secondary teachers have extracurricular responsibilities that add to their workload. Various measuring formulas for assessing workload have been presented in the previous chapters. In the following sections of chapter 4, the recommendations and strategies for improving teacher workload are discussed. Various discussions assume that normal times for open schools are back in operation and that both teachers and students have returned to school.

IMPROVING THE TEACHER WORKLOAD PROBLEMS IN SCHOOL SETTINGS

Improving the teacher workload problem is considered to be the primary purpose of this book. The educational procedures for student learning tend to differ widely during the virus epidemic. Above and beyond getting better funding and hiring more teachers, chapter 4 presents additional steps and strategies that are recommended for improving teacher workload. The topic of school climate and its vital importance for improving teacher workload has been discussed previously. Other leadership activities and program revisions for improving teacher workload are presented in this chapter. In any case, resolving teacher workload problems is not an easy task. If it were, it most likely would have been resolved long ago.

GETTING HELP FROM THE AVAILABLE LITERATURE: MAYBE AND MAYBE NOT

The literature appears to be plentiful on the topic of the problems of teacher workload; helpfulness is not so plentiful. One workload reduction article stated at the outset that there were 16 ways to reduce teacher load along with a comment that 16 seems like a lot of tips. The writer was right, one good tip might have been helpful. Here are three really, really good ones: work with a "do less" partner, do less, and stop focusing on your weaknesses.

Our perspectives are focused on what the local school system can do to reduce teacher workload. One assertion from an article by teachwire (Harris, 2019) stated that it was the government that must address the teacher workload issues. Harris noted that the systematic issues behind excessive workload can only be tackled by the government. That will be the day! Counting on the government to settle the teacher workload issues is likened to having someone in the government calling on the telephone and telling you that you have an appointment set for getting your first virus vaccination. Didn't education have major problems with the "load" of governmental mandates during the Obama administration?

LOGICAL FIRST STEPS FOR OBTAINING PERSONAL HELP

What was the best source for gaining help/advice relative to your needs/problems over the years? Was the source a person or perhaps an activity that was quite successful? A family member? A friend? A teacher or another person whom you knew? Such "mentors" most likely have had similar workload experiences in their line of work. Asking for help is a sign of intelligence. One seeking help is not complaining, rather he or she is seeking advice for ways to get the best job done with less pressure and strain.

What about the importance of the responsibilities teachers are facing? One teacher reported that she simply "did not do" one of the so-called activities of her job. What were the outcomes of her not doing them? When asked this question, she wasn't ready to give an immediate response. It is not the purpose here to recommend not doing the tasks; rather it is of most importance for the worker to give serious attention to what really is important in the work at hand. One social studies teacher reported that he did not complete a lesson plan for a class one day. What were the consequences of his actions? He said that it was one of the best classes that he had instructed so far in the school semester.

To what extent do you have control over your work responsibilities? A great deal? Little or none? When control is in place, what actions can be taken to reduce the job pressure? Do you have the option of saying "no"? In many cases, the teacher has the option of saying, "No, I appreciate the importance of the request, but present responsibilities take priority at this time." Or, be truthful by responding, "I can't participate at this time, but please keep me in mind." In case of agency mandates, do your best to comply. Nevertheless, give serious thought to what you are doing relative to the request and report those activities as fits the case. You are saying "no" but saying it indirectly. Self-control is the belief that humans are intelligent and have the capacity of implementing practices that facilitate their ability to improve.

The foregoing comments are not stated to encourage an action of not doing the job, but rather to keep clearly in mind that not every "mandate" or job is absolutely essential; a change of procedure or a more informal session with students can often set the stage for creating closer student relationships and/or fostering an improved positive climate in the classroom.

GIVE ATTENTION TO SOME IMPORTANT SELF-CHECKS ON A TEACHER'S WORK ASSIGNMENT

The high importance of purpose and planning suggests that goals and objectives do loom important for effective student learning. It is quite common for individuals to prepare a daily listing of things to be accomplished. It also is quite common for individuals to ask themselves at the end of the day, "Just what were my accomplishments today?" Such a procedure often underscores the things that did not go so well that day. Helping oneself looms important. A high school principal used the procedure of a self-evaluation and stated that the procedure was the most important self-improvement activity that he has ever experienced over his 31 years of his involvement in school administration.

In brief, the school principal explained his 20-minute self-evaluation procedure as follows:

At the end of each school week, I find a quiet place at home and examine the calendar of activities/events that took place during the last week. What activities and events were of most importance? Which activities and events served the best purposes? What results went well and why were they so successful? Which results were not so successful and why? What did I do right in the instances when results were most positive? What might I have done better to resolve problems or answer the questions that were presented? What follow-up might be necessary at this point and time?

Airasian and Gullickson (1997) believe that there are several important criteria that must be met regarding the effectiveness of self-evaluation strategies. These authorities stated the following:

- *The teacher must have a commitment to practice and to his or her responsibility to understand, evaluate, and improve it. The initiative and desire for self-evaluation have to come from the teacher.
- *If self-evaluation is to be truly self-evaluation, the teacher must assume control of the self-evaluation process. In particular, the teacher must be the one who carries out reflection and makes the ultimate decision about his or her workload responsibilities.
- *Unless a teacher acknowledges responsibility for the possibility of being able to improve an area of practice, the self-evaluation process is unlikely to be carried out.

It is clear that teacher workload problems cannot be resolved by external parties alone. That is, the individual teacher must take special steps personally toward reaching an improvement. The following "principle" is interesting and the steps that it recommends might even work.

THE 80/20 RULE: WORK LESS AND ACHIEVE MORE—REALLY?

Core Sparker (2021) explained what has been termed the 80/20 rule for reducing one's workload and increasing the outputs. In brief, the 80/20 rule states that a small amount of input can contribute to a much larger output. The answer? Just cut out everything that does not contribute to the primary purpose to be achieved. After all, it is 20% of the work inputs that produce 80% of the productive results. The need is to cut the time spent on those things that do not contribute to the desired ends. In essence, the teacher is cutting out those work activities that actually do not contribute to his or her primary purposes; student learning is not enhanced.

As underscored by Core Sparker, when the individual person works ineffectively, he or she spends 80% of their time to gain 20% of their results. Of course, there are other considerations that come into play. For example, other authorities have pointed out the fact that the other 80% of success is due to psychology, mindset, beliefs, and emotions and only 20% is due to strategy which includes the specific steps needed to accomplish a result. Thus, the 80/20 rule is not a hard/fast rule, but one that encourages the worker to spend the majority of time on productive purposes: work that centers directly on the things that really matter.

The key is this. The individual needs to focus on which work tasks center on the most important purposes. Which activities/tasks are more likely to result in the desired success? These activities/tasks should be given priority. The teacher might be able to work less and achieve more. There is an old story about the man who arrived for his doctor's appointment. His doctor asked, "How may I help you?" The patient raised his arm and said, "Doc, when I do this my arm hurts!" The doctor said, "Well, don't do that!"

POSSIBLE CHANGES

In one informal session with secondary school teachers, we asked teachers how they have improved their workload. A few of their responses follow:

"Instead of assigning homework each day, use 10 minutes of class time to have three or four groups of students do a selected assignment and assess it orally in class. If the students respond to the assignment correctly in class, an understanding of the class material has been demonstrated. If not, open the next class period with a planned review of the main lesson."

"Use the last 5 minutes of the class for asking two or three questions and call on students to respond. Note those areas where student answers are not on target. Start the next lesson by reviewing the material in question. Avoid using written quizzes and/or homework that requires marking."

"Use the last five to ten minutes of the class to have groups of four students discuss a question of importance for the lesson at hand. Ask one of the groups to report on their response. Briefly comment on the students' responses. Each student group will be able to reflect on the 'best' response. The activity is not for grading purposes, but rather for assessing the students' learning of the lesson at hand." Note that no grade marking of oral responses is required. Student learning is of first importance. In a few minutes, the teacher is able to assess and evaluate the extent of student learning and adjust the following lesson(s) accordingly.

WHAT OTHER STEPS CAN BE TAKEN TO REDUCE TEACHER WORKLOAD?

First and foremost, school leaders must be able to assess and evaluate the workloads of each teacher. The use of the various teacher workload formulas, presented in earlier chapters, would be of most help. For example, the

Douglass Teacher Load Formula and the Norton/Bria Elementary School Teacher Load Formula, discussed in chapter 2, would serve to provide the status/equity of workload assignments in the school. Workloads of teachers are commonly self-imposed. Consider the workload case of teacher, Donn White.

THE CASE OF THE HIGH SCHOOL'S BAND/ORCHESTRA TEACHER

Dr. Donn White was the band/orchestra teacher for Lafayette Senior High School. Parents of the student in the high school had been "pushing" for a new beginning orchestra class at the school. Principal Wallace Brown arranged a meeting with Dr. White to discuss the matter. Dr. White's first response was to point out his already heavy workload and "argued" against adding any new orchestra classes.

In turn, Principal Brown shared his recent teacher load assessment study with Dr. White. The study, which used the Douglass Teacher Load Formula, revealed that Dr. White had a teacher load index of 36.4 which was below the median of the entire faculty index of 42.4. In fact, Dr. White's perspective of his workload included the many events/performances that he was scheduling for his bands especially outside of school performances.

Dr. White was quick to note that his workload was being stressful due to his agreeing to lead his orchestra or band in the many community programs that were scheduled each year. He became aware that his actual teacher workload at the school was fair and equitable. It was his outside-the-school commitments that were adding to his work activities.

School leaders should administer a teacher load assessment each year in order to identify inequities and other factors that are inhibiting the positive performances of faculty personnel. Once such an assessment has been completed, the school leader can evaluate the results and make any changes that are in the best interests of the teacher, the students, and the school. As previously noted, the workload issue in schools can serve to inhibit job satisfaction and effectiveness of faculty members in the school. Authorities recommend that teachers give serious consideration to student assignments that require marking and those assignments that do not. Of course, using the assignments that do not require marking serves toward reducing the workload.

In other student assignments, the use of peer-assessments might be most appropriate. This strategy is closely related to collaborative learning that has been promoted for enriching student learning during the past two decades. Almost every teacher will recall the time when the student was "ordered" to do his or her own work. No help from other students, and assigned homework was not to be "done" by other members at home. Today, collaborative learning is promoted. Some authorities have recommended that a "no-marking" policy be adopted. The use of the strategies previously noted for reducing workload and the use of technology that fosters live feedback can serve to reduce the great amounts of marking commonly required by the school teacher.

CREATING A WELL-BEING STRATEGY IN THE SCHOOL

In chapter 3, the importance of fostering a positive school climate was discussed in-depth. Research reports have pointed out that a large percent of teachers do not feel that they have enough guidance about mental health and well-being at work. Along with the importance of a positive school climate, building a positive school culture is essential as well. As defined earlier in chapter 2, *school climate* is the collective personality of the school or school system. It is the atmosphere that prevails as characterized by the social and professional interactions of people. On the other hand, *culture* is the set of important beliefs and values that members of the school system share. Culture is more normative than climate in the sense that it is a reflection of the shared values, beliefs, and underlying assumptions of school members across an array of organizational dimensions that include but go beyond interpersonal relationships.

CREATING THE WELL-BEING OF THE TEACHING FACULTY

Creating a well-being strategy can be enhanced by building a positive school culture. School principals and school leadership teams (SLT) must help foster a positive school culture by valuing teachers in the implementation of the purposes of the school, its primary values, and how these values are permeated into the atmosphere of the school's program activities. Teachers need to be apprised of their importance in the implementation of programs and activities that are founded on important values and beliefs. How the teacher is valued and how they are recognized for their good work are essentials for building the positive school culture needed in the school environment.

Such support is not always a difficult task. Rather, a note of praise most often is especially appreciated. "Miss O'Brien, your contributions to the student after-school program activities have proven to be especially successful."

"Emory, with your initiative the school's new efforts to gain parental involvement has been a success." "Nancy, as senior class president, you have done an amazing job of gaining student participation in our after-school student help program."

Just give it a little thought. Each person most commonly is able to recall a positive comment by a faculty member that is remembered overtime. Such positiveness builds relationships, improves the climate, and lessens the workload problems facing school personnel.

The improvement of teacher workload must be considered as being of high importance in the governance policies of the school district. A school policy looms important since it centers on what the school district wants to achieve. Have you ever seen a school district policy that centered on promoting a better work/life balance for teachers? In most cases, the "school policy" is expressed more like an administrative regulation. That is, it sets forth the load specifications for teacher service as opposed to expressing the purposes that the school district is working to achieve regarding equitable teacher workload assignments.

A VOLUME OF IDEAS AND RECOMMENDATIONS FOR IMPROVING TEACHER WORKLOAD

One relatively recent recommendation for reducing the strain and stress of teaching and in turn improving student learning is to adopt *flexible teaching*. Flexible teaching is allowing class lessons to have a much lower structure by letting discussions and thoughts play out, then following them to see where they go. Instead of following the lesson plan, the teacher pursues the instruction depending on what comes to the floor and then capitalizing on student inquiry–based learning where by the teacher serves as a facilitator.

The teacher is prepared to move with the minds of the students in the classroom. The teacher serves as a guide, facilitator, and responder in dealing with different student abilities, needs, and interests. The teacher does provide some form of structure that serves to bring the discussions/thoughts sensibly together. The teacher's "control" is vested in his or her ability to provide controlled guidance.

But what does all of these strategies have to do with improving teacher workload? Such actions tend to lessen conflicts that commonly occur and facilitate the Primary chapter goal: to set forth the recommended practices/strategies for improving teacher workload in the schools by fostering the conditions of a healthy school climate. It lessens the time being spent on problems and encourages cooperation among the faculty, staff, and students.

Teaching effectiveness promotes student interest and flexible teaching serves in a positive way to increase student interest. Some teachers have reported that the more flexibly a teacher "teaches," the better the chances that student participation is increased. The principle of meeting students' interests and needs has always been voiced as a primary purpose. Flexible teaching is focused on the implementation of this principle.

ASSESS AND EVALUATE—YES, THE WORKLOAD REQUIREMENTS CAN BE REDUCED

Can you name several teacher activities that do not add to the teacher's workload? New mandates/requirements for teacher reporting, new implementation of technological services, extended requirements for student assessments/evaluations, and other extensions related to impact-reporting have continued to add to the teacher's workload rather than helping to reduce it. The literature on teacher workload and its inhibiting factors has been in the news for long periods of time. In the following section, strategies for reducing such teacher workloads are discussed.

Although there is a volume of reasons why teachers are leaving the profession, topping the list of reasons why they are leaving, according to nearly every survey, is the workload that they are having to carry. What is needed to meet this crisis? One area that is commonly noted focuses on administrative/leadership practices. Leaders must, first and foremost, take special means to examine the demands being made through their offices for meeting the high-stakes accountability mandates including testing, ongoing change, and the school's communication measures.

The volumes of email messages that must first be read and then responded to are one example. Is there any control on how many emails that teachers receive each day? It is reasonable to contend that a teacher expends 10 minutes each day reading his/her emails and 20 minutes a day responding to them. That is, the teacher spends 30 minutes each day and 150 minutes each week reading and responding to email messages. This task adds 2.5 hours a week to the teacher's workload. The primary point here is that, although the time spent on emailing might be highly productive, on the other hand, it might be a questionable addition to the workload of the teacher. The important question that must be answered includes "Is the time given to emailing proving to be an effective communication method that serves the school's educational goals and objectives?"

A second Bromley review factor is that of school scheduling. He asks, of how might the calendar add to a busy teacher's workload burden? More specifically; just how is the school's calendar of events affecting the workload of the teacher? For example, just how do the various calendar events (e.g., PTA and other parents' meetings, student events, school plays, sport's activities, open houses, and awards meetings and other such events) add to the workload of teachers in the school? Are the purposes of such scheduled events supporting the purposes set forth in the school's "policy" statements? Not only do such events add to the workload of teachers, but their actual accomplishments for student learning are seldom assessed and evaluated.

The topic of marking and its effect on teacher load has been mentioned previously in the chapter. Nevertheless, the question of purpose is answered by the extent to which the assessment will serve to improve student learning and the extent to which it adds to the workload of faculty personnel. How will it benefit the educational program and help students improve their learning?

The focus here is student learning. If the assessment is merely to satisfy a report or justify the time and effort being devoted to an activity, it should be set aside. Is the time and effort to be devoted to the assessment justified in relation to its potential for improving student learning while not adding unwisely to the workload of the professional staff? But how should these questions be answered before the project is initiated? If projected purposes and outcomes cannot be validly projected, they should be set aside or implemented in a planned pilot program before expanding throughout the school system.

It looms important for the school community to be informed/knowledgeable about the program for assessment to be implemented. It must be made clear as to how the program implementation will have an important program improvement without adding initially to the workload of the teaching staff.

STUDENT BEHAVIOR AND ITS IMPACT ON TEACHER WORKLOAD: WHAT CAN BE DONE TO RESOLVE THIS PROBLEM?

Greenwood (2019, October) reports that 70% of teachers have considered quitting due to poor student behavior. He also contends that managing student behavior is one of the most constraining parts of a teacher's job. Empirical research has shown that poor student behavior can provoke mental health issues revealed by pressure and strain that drain the physical strength and well-being of the teacher. Isn't it appropriate to mention the time that most teachers spend on behavior management in-service programs?

Give thought to the time that a teacher must spend in dealing with student behavior problems. In some cases, it is a matter of the "lost time" by having to sit with the student in the classroom or other behavior areas after school, keeping an accurate record/report of the incident(s) relative to the student's behavior violations, taking time to confer with parents by telephone or in person, spending time "mentoring" the student on matters related to the behavioral record, and spending additional time for following up on other professional matters that were "set aside" due to the time that had to be spent on the one or more behavioral problems faced.

MAKING AN EFFORT TO REDUCE THE WORKLOAD DUE TO POOR STUDENT BEHAVIOR

When the school climate is healthy, student behavioral problems are lessened. When the rules for the games and activities on the school playground are determined largely by the students, playground problems commonly are lessened as well. We submit that student behavioral policy and regulations should be determined with student involvement as well. The following light-bulb experience is a case in point.

THE CASE OF THE DISSATISFIED STUDENT

Scott Carson was a senior class student at Lafayette Senior High School. He was active in class activities and participated in every sport that the school supervised. He commonly was on the honor roll scholastically and had been selected as the editor of the school newspaper and of the senior class yearbook.

He had become disgruntled for some reason for several days. The English literature teacher, Mrs. Flowers, noted Scott's "attitude" in one class session and addressed Scott by saying, "OK, Scott, you have been acting somewhat disgruntled for few classes now. Your uncooperative behavior has been somewhat disruptive. So, if you have something to say just come to the front of the class and say it."

Scott stood and walked to the front of the class that consisted of senior classmates. He opened his remarks by saying the following:

> In just three months, our class will be seated at our high school graduation ceremonies and a speaker will be telling us that we have had a solid education and would soon be in roles as leaders of our communities. He will underscore the fact that we have been academically and socially educated to take over the leadership in communities around the nation and the world.

Scott went on to say that he felt that the speaker would be wrong, that the school personnel had not given students the important responsibilities and opportunities to develop the leadership knowledge and skills needed for such success. He went on to say that a few days ago three of us were working on a piece during the noon hour for the school newspaper and typing it in the school typing room. The typing teacher came into the room and asked what we were doing. She insisted that we shouldn't be in the room without proper supervision. She went on to say that these are expensive typing machines and you have no business using them without someone here to supervise.

Scott also commented on the nature of the rules that senior students had to follow. For example, he noted that students had to ask permission to go to the restroom. We carry a permission slip to be out of class. We sit in class in five straight rows of five students, just like we did in first grade. Many of us will enter college next year. I don't expect to witness any of these constraints in college which is just a few months away. Several new student rules have been imposed this year. I can't remember ever being asked my opinion about them. Have any of you? I don't think that I will need a pass to use the bathroom or have to go to the college dean to get permission to get into class if I am a bit late. As seniors, we are treated much like we were treated in elementary school.

Mrs. Flowers, said Scott, "You asked me to stand and speak up about my feelings. This I have done."

At that point and time, Mrs. Flowers, the teacher, got up from her desk and left the classroom. In just a few minutes she returned accompanied by the school principal. Just what the school principal said to the class is not remembered. But what happened the next day at the school is well remembered. The very first student council at Lafayette High School was initiated. Representatives of the student body worked with school personnel in the development of a Student Governance Policy and Procedures statement. Council representatives from each school grade were elected as were the president, vice president, and financial manager for the council.

The history shows that the Lafayette High School was closed seven years after the first student council was implemented. But from all the communication that surrounded the first council and its continuation for the next seven years, student satisfaction, student academic performance, and student behavioral records all improved positively over the remaining years of its existence. It is reasonable to expect that the overall school climate improved as the student council began to function.

With the improvement in student climate/behavior, it is quite reasonable that teacher workload, related to student behavior, was improved as well. It also seems to be a reasonable conclusion that, ultimately, the improvement of student behavior must come from the behavioral decisions of the student. The strategy is to focus on ways in which the student(s) can be a major part of behavior-problem solutions.

As a sidenote of the foregoing story and at a later time, Mrs. Flowers (not the teacher's real name) became the school principal in a middle school in Lincoln, Nebraska. Interestingly enough, the former student, Scott Carson (not his real name), became a school district administrator in the Lafayette school district (not its real name) and worked directly with Mrs. Flowers in the same school system for several years.

OTHER WAYS AND MEANS FOR REDUCING STUDENT BEHAVIORAL PROBLEMS

Greenwood (2021) set forth four important recommendations for reducing the impact of student behavior management workload for the school staff. As noted previously, Greenwood recommended the development and implementation of a student behavior policy which is consistently communicated and reinforced by all school stakeholders: in addition, a centralized praise and detention system to reinforce positive school behavior. That is, find the best ways in which to recognize positive student behavior which commonly is best recorded by a simple positive recognition of positive behavior and positive relationships.

Being aware of the behavior issues that are occurring in the school climate is important. Taking care of "trouble spots" before real problems happen serves a positive purpose. After-school retentions, dismissal from classes, and other "penalty" provisions are not only ineffective behavioral strategies, but also wastes of teacher time. Teachers should explain the class expectations for student behavior and be consistent in their enforcement. When it comes right down to it, students favor a positive class climate as well. In one instance, a teacher in Lafayette High School had to leave the classroom. She asked the class to "assume" the responsibility for class talking/behavior. One student spoke up after the teacher left the room; class members took care of the talking immediately.

AFTER ALL IS SAID AND DONE

When all is said and done, at this point and time, we really do not know much at all about reducing teacher workload. Virtually no important empirical or basic research has been done on the topic. That is, all of the so-called research on teacher load comes about by showing the results of teacher surveys regarding conditions of load being faced and the extent to which various load factors are causing stress and dissatisfaction. We were unable to find one research study whereby a workload improvement plan had been implemented and the results were studied scientifically as to the extent that the program improved workload results.

One source reported that it had developed a "Reducing Teacher Workload" tool kit. Each section of the tool kit is paired with actionable advice and resources that teachers can instantly apply to better help them deal with excessive workload (apparently how to deal with it, not to help resolve it). The results of the use/applications of the tool kit were not reported. However, the article did go on to tell us about the major problems of teacher workload: date management, curriculum planning and resources, and communication.

Let us examine the recommendations of Satchel for reducing workload due to data management.

According to Satchel (2021), the way to reduce the impact that data management has on workload is as follows. First, audit the data you collect to assess its worth. Second, debunk myths associated with data management. Third, ensure data meets the requirements outlined by the workload advisory group. Fourth, ensure the technology you use aids data management and doesn't add to it. Got it? No information was given regarding just how each recommendation was to be accomplished and how the solution did not require a great deal of workload time for some school personnel.

It is clear that there are no easy solutions to the teacher load problem. Current workload problems have changed due to the changes in educational programing due to the virus epidemic. Teachers are leaving the profession in increasing numbers. Attempts to open schools have failed due to the fact that, in many cases, teachers have failed to show up for duty. A recent article in the *Arizona Republic* (2021, February 2) was titled, "Teacher Shortage Plagues Arizona." Over 1,000 teachers had resigned since the school year began. One Arizona teacher continued teaching and her next job paid 25% more, came with a stipend, and reimbursed her for rent. The new job was in China! Just a thought. Does America really believe that education is one of its highest priorities?

RECOMMENDATIONS FOR REDUCING TEACHER LOAD: WHAT DO TEACHERS SAY?

In an attempt to answer the title question above, we asked school principals to tell us what they recommended to be done to improve the teacher workload problems facing school in American. Seven specific recommendations led their responses. We asked the teachers the following question: If you were the school principal of your school, what would you try to do to improve the teacher load situation in your school community? Seven specific recommendations led the responses. We note that we did not ask the participating teachers to present their ideas as to how each recommendation was to be accomplished. Yet, some respondents did set forth various steps that should be taken to improve the workload situation. Seven "improvement areas" were reported: (a) securing additional personnel, (b) improvement of administrative management, (c) improvement of the scheduling of school programs, (d) improvement of the school plant, (e) increase of teachers including extra pay for extra duties, (f) general comments that the principal was doing all he/she could do, and (g) satisfactory conditions existed.

A CONCLUSION

Although the foregoing information does not give us sufficient information regarding how the teacher workloads can be improved, it certainly underscores many of the problem areas whereby improvements can be made. For example, in entry 3a in Table 4.1, "fair and equal treatment of teachers in various work assignments" can quite readily be determined by implementing the Douglass Teacher Load Formula. We have that strategy at hand.

Using it in each school semester will result in an improvement of teacher teaching and cooperative workloads. What is needed? The need is vested in using the formula. Inequality of teacher workloads, including inequality of cooperative work assignments, can be assessed, evaluated, and revised according to the workload results. Today's technology can be used to calculate the workload information of each teacher in just a few minutes. Little if any additional work is required on the part of the teacher. A member of the support staff in the school, when well trained, could complete this task in a very short period of time.

SUMMING IT ALL UP: WHAT HAVE WE EMPHASIZED IN THE BOOK'S FOUR CHAPTERS

In undertaking necessary adjustment of teacher load in the nation's schools, the following basic procedures and considerations appear to be desirable:

1. Priority attention should be given as to what constitutes an equitable body of assignments for the school teacher. In determining this equity, attention must be given to all of the factors that make up teacher workload. Facts should be available in a form that makes analysis "easy" to complete. Using a recognized formula for assessing teacher load is one way to gain specific evidence of the status of a teacher's workload. Workload calculations for all teachers provide the school leaders with evidence of inequities that exist and information that helps them avoid giving the heaviest workloads to new teaching personnel and to the school's best

Table 4.1 Recommendations by High School Teachers on What Principals Might Do to Improve Teacher Load

Recommendations	All Teachers Percent
1. Try to secure additional personnel	
a. More teachers, lower pupil-teacher ratio	29.6%
b. More clerical help	4.3%
c. Assistance for monitorial jobs, study halls	2.0%
d. Other personnel such as more full-time supervisors, counselors, coordinators	1.2%
2. Try to improve the administrative management of the school	
a. Recommendations referring to general school policies, such as curriculum, selection of teachers, substitute teachers	7.9%
b. Fewer outside activities, fewer meetings, fewer extracurricular activities	4.0%
c. Considerate or democratic attitude, joint planning, less discord	3.2%
d. More textbooks and supplies	1.6%
e. Better planning of school activities	.4%
f. Better leadership of school principal in handling student behavior	.8%
g. Better grouping of pupils	3.6%
h. Increased guidance services	3.6%
3. Try to improve the scheduling of the school program	
a. Fair and equal treatment of teachers in various work assignments	15.8%
b. Proving for a free period or other free time for each teacher every day	7.5%
c. Assigning teachers in their major subject areas	3.6%
d. Change the time for various subjects according to their subjects taught	.8%
4. Try to improve the school plant	
a. Try to get more classrooms, have less crowding	11.9%
5. Other suggestions such as	
a. Increase finances, increase salaries, pay for extra duties	6.7%
6. Comments	
a. Nothing principal can do	1.2%
b. Principal doing all that can be done	5.1%
7. Satisfactory conditions exist	22.9%

teachers. When this recommendation is not followed, new teachers and the school's best teachers commonly are lost to the profession.

2. Rather than leaving the teacher workload decision to each school principal, a sound school board policy with appropriate administrative regulations must be determined by the local school board. A policy sets forth the goals/objectives of the workload provisions for the school teachers in the system. Cooperatively developed administrative regulations answer the question as to how the policy is to be administered. Empirical workload studies have revealed that first-year teachers and the school's best teachers commonly are carrying the heaviest teaching workloads. This research fact underscores the reason that nearly 25% of all first-year teachers quit the profession after

the first year of teaching. Giving the school's best teachers the heaviest workload leads to the loss of quality personnel as well.
3. In any effort to improve the workload problem in the school district, the involvement of teacher personnel is a "must" involvement practice. As previously noted, solutions to the teacher workload problems in a school district ultimately will depend on the common collaborate decision-making process of the school board and teacher associations. Both of these professional groups want what is best for students. Both groups have their ideas/opinions about the status of teacher workloads in the schools. Both groups want what is best for students and student learning. Both need to work cooperatively in ameliorating and ultimately resolving the ongoing workload problems.
4. Any attempt to apply many of the recommendations for resolving the teacher workload problems in America's schools is inhibited with the current COVID-19 epidemic facing America and the world. Even with virtual learning methods, the epidemic moves on and (as of February 8, 2021), the top headline read as follows: *Student Testing to Return in April.* Testing results are to test how students have progressed—or regressed—academically since the pandemic began.
5. On the basis of teacher recommendations and conclusions drawn from the literature, ideal solutions to the teacher workload problem will come about only by securing adequate financial support for the school so as to make possible the employing of more qualified teachers and other employees and providing funds for the construction of better school plants, thus reducing the teacher load of individual teachers. If indeed, education in America is essential for the continuation of a democratic society, the support of a free enterprise system, and the best opportunity for a fair and equal chance in life for each individual, it must be among the highest of priorities among the many priorities that are important in our country.

CHAPTER 4 QUIZ

Directions: Circle the correct response to each of the following multiple-choice questions.

1. The 80/20 rule states that
   a. 80% of new teachers will produce only 20% of the positive school objectives.
   b. 80% of the school's teachers will produce 20% of the positive school objectives.

    c. it is 20% of the input that produces 80% of the results.
    d. it is 80% of the input that produces 20% of the results
    e. none of the above.
2. First and foremost, school leaders must be able to
    a. get all teachers to give 100% to their work responsibilities.
    b. assess and evaluate the workload of each teacher.
    c. see to it that all the teachers are really "on the job."
    d. get the most of each teacher's ability.
    e. none of the above.
3. The Douglass teacher Load Formula was designed to help school administrators
    a. check on the knowledge of new teachers relative to their understanding of student learning in larger classes of students.
    b. and teachers gain a better understanding of their overall job responsibilities.
    c. assess and evaluate the workload of all teachers in the school.
    d. assign teachers to classroom and extra duty responsibilities.
    e. none of the above.
4. Flexible teaching is
    a. teaching five classes one day and three the next day, and one on the third day.
    b. using all varieties of learning styles.
    c. completing homework in school and schoolwork at home.
    d. allowing class lessons to have a much lower structure by letting discussion play out.
    e. none of the above.
5. If teacher self-evaluation is to be truly self-evaluation
    a. the teacher must gain control of the process.
    b. the process must be easily accomplished.
    c. the process must be on his or her success level.
    d. the school principal must approve the process and give school time to do the process.
    e. none of the above.
6. When school climate is healthy,
    a. all students get higher grades.
    b. teacher workload is improved.
    c. teacher workload changes, but not always for the better.
    d. for some unknown reason, teachers' workloads increase.
    e. none of the above.
7. According to school teachers, one best way to reduce teacher load is to
    a. give the class more books and instructional resources.
    b. hire more qualified teachers.
    c. better plan school activities.
    d. increase guidance services.
    e. none of the above.

8. Creating a well-being strategy in the school can be enhanced by
   a. having faculty social events on a regular basis.
   b. reducing parental visitations.
   c. building a positive school culture.
   d. giving extra pay for work done at home.
   e. none of the above.
9. School climate and school culture are
   a. synonymous.
   b. related to the pupil's family background.
   c. different by definition.
   d. the same by definition
   e. none of the above.
10. One way to improve teacher workload is to
    a. focus on work tasks that the teacher likes to do.
    b. have the students mark/grade their own school homework.
    c. decrease or completely stop all student written assignments.
    d. focus on what work tasks center on the most important purposes and give them priority.
    e. none of the above.

ANSWERS TO THE QUIZ

The answer to question #1 is "c," #2 is "b," #3 is "c,'" #4 is "d," #5 is "a," #6 is "b," #7 is "b," #8 is "c," #9 is "c," #10 is "d."

QUIZ SCORING RESULTS

10–9 correct answers: ***** five stars
8–7 correct answers: **** four stars
6–5 correct answers: *** three stars
4–3 correct answers: ** two stars
2–1 correct answers: * one star

KEY CHAPTER IDEAS AND RECOMMENDATIONS

- *Resolving the teacher workload problems in the nation's schools is a most difficult situation at best. The current COVID-19 epidemic has added negatively to the teacher's workload difficulties as well.
- *Assessing and evaluating the workload of each teacher is essential. Just listening to teacher complaints about workload serves little value toward

their resolution. Using a workload formula, such as the Douglass Teacher Load Formula, has been a successful strategy in many schools nationally. Inequities are identified, and in some cases can be corrected for the benefit of the teacher and the school climate.
- *The well-being of the school faculty looms important relative to fostering a positive school climate. A positive school climate facilitates teacher workload improvement.
- *Teacher workload problems have been found to be causing the loss of hiring and retaining teacher personnel.
- *The increasing use of marking, data collection, and student testing are among the activities that have increased the workload of the teaching staff. These activities can and should be curtailed. The question to ask is, "How does this activity serve to improve the teacher workload problem?"
- *Poor student behavior is a leading cause of teacher workload. Student behavior can be improved. When steps are implemented to do so, teacher workload will be improved immensely.
- *The literature is complete with the identification of factors that cause teacher workload problems. Effective treatments for resolving teacher workload problems are not so prevalent. Far more attention must be given to the implementation of treatment factors that serve to reduce teacher workload.
- *It is clear that teacher workload has been a national school problem historically. The nation's presidents and other authorities have spoken of the importance of education for many reasons. Until education is adequately financed, teacher workload will remain on the list of the nation's problems. Yes, the national government and state offices are budgeting large sums of money for educational support. However, teacher salaries remain unattractive and do not encourage the hiring and retention of teachers in our nation's schools. The result is the lack of teachers for the nation's schools and the loss of teachers that have decided to leave the profession.

CHAPTER REFERENCES

Airasian, P. W., & Gullickson, A. R. (1997). *Teacher Self-Evaluation Tool Kit*. Microfilm Book, ERIC Clearing House.
Arizona Republic Newspaper (2021, January 8). *Teacher Shortage in Arizona. Section, B-1,* Phoenix, AZ.
Bromley, M. (2020, June 10). Reducing teacher workload: Four key areas to review. From the web: https://www.headteacher-update.com/best-practice-article/reducing-teacher-workload-for-key-areas-to-review/227822/
Core Sparker (2021, January 28). *What is 80/20 Rule About? From the web:* https://coresparker.wordpress.com/2017/10/13/what-is-2080-rule-about/

Greenwood, B. (2019). *The Complete Guide to Reducing Teacher Workload.* satchel: From the web: https://blog.teamsatchel.com/the-complete-guide-to-reducing-teacher-workload

Harris, T. (2019, November 22). Teacher Workload—Government must address the issues. *teachwire.* From the web: https://www. teachwire.net/news/teacher-workload-the-government-must-address-the-issues

About the Author

Dr. M. Scott Norton has served as a secondary school teacher of mathematics; coordinator of curriculum for the Lincoln, Nebraska School District; assistant superintendent for instruction; and superintendent of schools in Salina, Kansas; before joining the University of Nebraska as professor and vice-chair of the Department of Educational Administration and Supervision. Later he served as professor and chair of the Department of Educational Administration and Policy Studies at Arizona State University where he is currently professor emeritus.

His primary research and instruction areas include educational leadership, human resources administration, teaching methods, governance policy, the assistant school principalship, competency-based administration, the school principalship, research methods, theory, organizational development, organizational change, organizational climate, and educational program improvement. He has published widely in national journals in the areas of teaching/instructional methods, organizational climate, gifted student programs, great teachers, student retention, organizational change, and others. He has published widely on a variety of educational topics for Rowman and Littlefield Publishers.

Dr. Norton has received several state and national awards honoring his services and contributions to the field of education and educational administration including awards from the American Association of School Administrators, the University Council for Educational Administration, the Arizona School Administrators Association, the Nebraska School Administrators Association, the Arizona Educational Research Association, the Arizona State College of Education Dean's Award for Distinguished Service to the Field, and the Arizona Information Service, and the award for service as president of the College of Education Faculty Association. He presently is serving as a member of the Arizona State University Emeritus College.

Dr. Norton's state and national leadership positions have included services as executive director of the Nebraska Association of School Administrators, member of the Board of Directors for the Nebraska Congress of Parents and Teachers, president of the Nebraska Council of Teachers of Mathematics, president of the Arizona School Administrators Higher Education Division, member of the Arizona School Administrators Board of Directors, staff associate for the University Council for Educational Administration, treasurer of the University Council for School Administration, state representative for the Nebraska Association of Secondary School Principals, member of the Board of Editors for the American Association of School Public Relations, and member of the governance council for the Arizona State University Emeritus College.

www.ingramcontent.com/pod-product-compliance
Lightning Source LLC
Chambersburg PA
CBHW032030230426

43671CB00005B/268